ALIEN GODDESS

ALIEN GODDESS
UFOs, AI, and the Goddesses of Ascension

Dr. Joanna Kujawa

Alien Goddess: UFOs, AI, and the Goddesses of Ascension

Dr. Joanna Kujawa

Tradepaper ISBN: 978-1-958921-74-6
Electronic ISBN: 978-1-958921-75-3

Library of Congress Control Number: 2025943211

Published by Haniel Press
An Imprint of Sacred Stories Publishing, Fort Lauderdale, FL

Printed in the United States of America

CONTENTS

AN INVITATION TO THE DETECTIVE JOURNEY OF OUR LIVES

What if the beings we call aliens meet us in the mystical spaces of our consciousness that traverse the boundaries between different realities? Is it possible that it's us reaching out to ourselves from the future with a warning about the consequences of choosing technology over our humanity? Can we find the tools for ascension encoded in the ancient goddesses' mythologies?

Alien Goddess: UFOs, AI, and the Goddesses of Ascension is not only a book; it's an invitation to a detective journey that can determine the trajectory of our lives. We embark on an investigation of the deepest and too often ignored undercurrents of our reality, which is much more layered than the powers-to-be would like us to believe. We are not solely material beings, and our minds are not just logical algorithms without a meaning. Our lives have multidimensional undercurrents that, under the right circumstances, open the doors to other realities of much greater possibilities for ourselves and our world.

Why are these realities hidden from us and what can we do to access them?

Alien Goddess attempts to answer these questions by taking you along on my detective journey to find the remedy to this situation. As a spiritual detective and scholar, I invite you to join me in this investigation. *Alien Goddess* does not just present you with research into these fascinating topics; it also takes you along on this journey, step by step, and shares my firsthand visions and personal experiences. Together, we will investigate both personal and documented experiences of UFOs and anomalous encounters with other beings. These encounters usually occur in liminal space between material and spiritual realities and might be experienced as abductions, lucid dreaming, or visitations. They often have a message for us—a message that we are entering a dangerous path.

As we examine UFOs as anomalous encounters, we learn that some of the most significant encounters, both collective and individual, are with a female, goddess-like figure who carries a message of hope. In *Alien Goddess*, we thoroughly investigate a few such phenomena, including the most well-known and mysterious one, which occurred in Fatima, Portugal, in 1917. We will also look into Chris Bledsoe's visitations from the White Lady as well as some abduction stories where a female alien transfers warning messages in an erotic act with a human.

What is her message to us?

This message became clearer to me after I observed the rapid development and the insistent temptation of the public with Artificial Intelligence. In *Alien Goddess*, we investigate recent attempts at converging spirituality with technology and the push for technology as a means of replacing humanity. Ideologies such as transhumanism and posthumanism promote either merging humanity with technology or replacing humanity with synthetic bodies and mechanistically focused minds. The same ideologies imply that our consciousness is not too different from computer programming and, as such, might be transferred to a robotic body. They tempt us with mechanical immortality and prophesize the age of spiritual machines that will replace us.

Alien Goddess boldly claims that the rational-logical mind is only a part of a broader and much deeper consciousness that is available to us, and that there is a staged attempt to convince us to give up that consciousness for the sake of technological advancement. It proposes that the antidote to this situation can be found in a wisdom we abandoned long ago in the mythologies of the descent and ascent of the Goddess. When we study the stories of *The Descent of Inanna*, the Eleusinian Mysteries, *The Gospel of Mary Magdalene*, or *Pistis Sophia*, we are faced with the same warning. In each myth, the descent is caused by external trickery or deception, and the ascent comes with help from above.

Yet, *Alien Goddess* does more than just investigate the ancient myths of descent. It also offers the tools for ascension that were encoded in those stories. In this way, *Alien Goddess* helps us understand why we allow ourselves to be deceived as it guides us in the process of ascension.

Why *Alien Goddess*?

The Goddess wisdom is the undercurrent of the book, both her presence and the lack of her presence. The lack of the awareness of her presence in our minds creates perceptions of reality that are mechanistic and devoid of soul and meaning, as well as the perceptions of reality that are based on those perceptions of reality. Discovering her presence in our awareness is a saving beacon of light as she presents a different way of perceiving reality: intuitive, holistic, and multidimensional. The awareness of that possibility can open the unseen door not only to other realities but also to our own spiritual evolution.

Yet do we recognize her as a part of our consciousness, that part that "hard" science seems to ignore—or are we already so disconnected from her that even after facing her in countless anomalous encounters or visitations, we consider her alien to us?

Who *exactly* is an alien goddess?

After writing of *The Other Goddess* (2022) I noticed a connection between different goddesses of the past. In *Alien Goddess*, as we investigate the possibilities more deeply, we find important clues as to who the alien goddess might be. For the true spiritual detectives out there, significant hints have been left at the end of each part of the book.

Why *Alien Goddess* now?

Alien Goddess bridges the teachings of ancient traditions and the future that we are building for ourselves and coming generations. It invites us to create that future consciously, from the best and highest parts of ourselves rather than from the misguided and unconscious beliefs that we hold about ourselves and the supremacy of technology over our own evolutionary potential. Our evolutionary potential is always present for us in the unique configuration of our spirit and biology—not in the logical, machine-like recesses of our minds that provide us with advanced technologies but destroy our souls.

There is nothing more urgent now than taking the wisdom encoded in the goddess myths to the future. We can learn from her warnings and use the spiritual tools she offers, or we can passively surrender to the option served to us by technological minds, a direction that might take us permanently to the place of disconnect from our own divinity.

We are standing at the edge of a turning point so quiet we may miss it—where the soul is being bargained away, not by war or catastrophe, but by our own fascination with artificial transcendence. This book isn't a thought experiment.

It's a last call.

PART 1
THE MESSENGERS: UFOs

UFOS, THE WHITE LADY, AND THE LADY OF FATIMA

I remember an early summer day in 1978 when my then best friend from school, Iwonka, came running up the stairs to the ninth-floor apartment where I lived with my mom. Iwonka lived two floors below. We were in the same class in school, sat at the same desk, and spent our lunch breaks together discussing all the wonderful adventures we anticipated after we graduated. We were both great fans of the original *Star Wars*, which we had seen multiple times in the local movie theatre, coincidentally called The Kosmos. We both wanted to be like Princess Leia: adventurous, wise, and goddess-like.

So, I was not terribly surprised when that evening, Iwonka ran up the stairs, completely out of breath, and announced that she, her little sister, and their parents had seen a flying saucer! They had spotted it above the fields of the rural area around our hometown of Lublin in eastern Poland. I thought this was very exciting and I was perhaps a little scared, but I believed her, even if nobody else did.

Iwonka promptly shared her sighting with our friends at school, particularly two boys who were our closest friends and who sat in front of us in class. They laughed, not in a mean way, but they told her she had seen

Star Wars too many times. No one made fun of her, but no one else believed her, either.

Since Iwonka and her family visited their relatives in the countryside quite often, they experienced a few more subsequent sightings. Each time, Iwonka swore that the spaceship, surrounded by orbs of light, was real. She was never disturbed by the generally amused responses she received when she detailed the sightings. Each time, she told us the same story: she was in a car with her parents and sister, driving back toward the city, when they saw a shiny object zigzagging across the sky with incredible speed. She would race to my mom's ninth-floor apartment, and we would stand on the balcony looking at the sky. Our flowery summer dresses were caressed by the evening breeze as we tried to conjure a sighting so that I could also see what she had seen. I wondered what messengers would reveal themselves through the unseen doors of Iwonka's sightings. But I never saw Iwonka's spaceship or its orbs.

Some years later, our paths parted. I left Poland for good and have lived in other countries, nudging at the mysteries of that door, not knowing that they would one day open to the revelation of the Goddesses of Ascension.

The possible confirmation of Iwonka's sighting did not come until much later in my life. In 2024, in subtropical Australia, I started writing this book. I decided to use the memory of my childhood friend as a bittersweet opening, although it had no significance except for a personal one. I was drinking my morning coffee with my husband, our dog Charlotte by my feet, and was preparing for my first interview on the topic of UFOs/UAPs (unidentified flying objects or unidentified anomalous phenomena) for this book. Suddenly something, some quiet voice, told me to google "UFO sightings in Poland."

The first result that showed up was the Emilcin sighting. It described a rather friendly abduction that occurred on May 10, 1978, in a rural area about thirty-five miles from Lublin, where I lived. Incidentally, Emilcin is just under thirty-five miles north of the village where Iwonka and her family had been visiting when they had had those multiple sightings. I was taken back to those days of my youth, when Iwonka and I had asked ourselves for the first time: Is this possible? And what did it mean for us?

It turns out the Emilcin abduction is a well-documented case. A Polish farmer, Jan Wolski, who was seventy-one years old at the time, had left for his fields on a horse-drawn cart in the early hours of the day. The rest is a narrative he recorded for those willing to hear his story. About halfway to his fields, his cart was stopped by two humanoid entities who spoke in a strange, non-human language. At first, he thought they might be tourists, which would have been just as unusual as an alien encounter, as hardly any tourists ever visited. It was still communist Poland, and we saw very few foreigners.

The visitors Wolski met were about 4.9 feet tall with slanted eyes and greenish gray skin. They took him up into a black with a grayish hue flying vessel that was hovering about sixteen feet above the field. He noticed that both the ship and the uniforms of the beings were the same color. He was also struck by the fact that there were no visible joints or mechanical features that could keep the ship together. Inside the ship, he noticed four black objects that appeared to be part of the walls and that made a constant humming noise. He described the walls as transparent, allowing him to see what was going on outside as well. The humanoid beings gestured for him to undress. They examined him with two round objects, then gestured again that he could put his clothes back on. They even offered him some nourishment that looked like metallic icicles, but Wolski refused.

The beings lowered him to the ground on an open lift of sorts and set him free. Wolski said he rode on his cart back to his house and told his sons and neighbors what had just happened. When they returned to the abduction area, the UFO was gone but the grass there was trodden and there were footprints leading in several directions.

A six-year-old boy from the same area said he had seen a strange object hovering above his family's barn about the same time of the day. He said it looked like it had been about to land there but then had moved away with great speed.

It is somehow reassuring that the locals did not make fun of Wolski's story and nobody in the press attempted to explain it as "swamp gas," as often happened in Western press when people reported UFO phenomena. In 2005, the Nautilus Foundation even erected a small monument in memoriam of the event with this inscription (in my translation into English): "On May 10, 1978, a UFO object landed here. One day, the truth will amaze us."

Is the story true? Iwonka's experiences could have been influenced by her *Star Wars* obsession–but it is extremely unlikely that Jan Wolski, living in a rural part of eastern Poland during communist times, had ever heard of either *Star Wars* or UFOs. My research into spirituality, which I began long before I became interested in UFOs, has taught me that the most significant experiences in our lives do not necessarily happen on the physical plane but rather in the liminal sphere.

Liminal, by definition, refers to a space that is "in-between," a threshold between worlds, a boundary, or a transitional space. These are the spaces or periods in our lives where we experience intuitions, insights, spiritual experiences, and the significant dreams we find difficult to convey in words. We might want to share this information with others but struggle to produce empirical evidence that anything happened. This is what I call the "unseen door"—a temporary opening in our consciousness that allows us to discern realities not available to us through our usual modes of perception.

It is not such a big stretch of imagination to see that the very reason why it is difficult to provide empirical evidence for the unusual experiences mentioned here is that they take us to the ephemeral world with which we are somehow familiar but which we seldom remember consciously. This world is not always of the same level of physicality that we are accustomed to in our regular, day-to-day reality. Providing evidence here is a little like trying to give physical proof of love to someone who has never experienced it.

With the exception of quantum physics, the way modern science approaches the liminal is to completely discredit it. In our current scientific paradigm, something has to be solely material to be considered real. This does not allow for any mystical space where an experience itself can be real even if it is not 100 percent material. Yet, in Wolski's case, there were some empirical details, such as the trodden grass and footprints, as well as a six-year-old boy who claimed to be an eyewitness.

The next matter for us to investigate is the connection between the experience of UFO phenomena and our personal beliefs. This might help us to explore that space, whether physical or other, in which these phenomena occur. But first, let's explore other events of the same nature and see what we can learn from them.

The White Lady

Two examples that will help us to investigate the unusual nature of some of the UFO sightings are Chris Bledsoe's experiences with what he calls the White Lady and the Lady of Fatima.

Probably the most well-known and coveted of UFO experiencers is Chris Bledsoe, who has appeared on endless podcasts and who recently published *The UFO of God: The Extraordinary True Story of Chris Bledsoe* (2023).

Like many UFO experiencers, Chris Bledsoe suffered humiliation in his own community in rural North Carolina as well as admonition from his religious congregation, which considers his experiences "demonic." Bledsoe's case was made even worse when representatives from MUFON (the Mutual UFO Network) showed curiosity about the unusual phenomena on his property which, in turn, led to Bledsoe being featured on the Discovery Channel in a derisive manner. This was especially difficult for him and his family, as the UFO community itself was ridiculing his experiences.

However, in a strange turn of events, his fortunes suddenly changed for the better and he now appears to be on good terms not only with academics but also with various governmental agencies and scientists who are normally reluctant to investigate this kind of phenomena.

The reason why Bledsoe has finally been considered a legitimate witness or experiencer by the authorities is due to four factors: 1) The phenomena around him have persisted for many years; 2) Several other people who visited his property had similar sightings (including some of the podcasters who interviewed him subsequently); 3) His personality; and 4) The consistency in the details of his experiences.

Although I was at first wary of his testimonies, I have to admit that Bledsoe does not appear to be someone wishing to manipulate public perceptions about anything. In fact, he gives the impression of being genuine to the point of being an *ingénue* or someone with disarming naiveté. The extreme detail in his descriptions would be difficult to maintain if he were referring to fictitious occurrences.

From the point of view of our detective work, Bledsoe's experiences are interesting because they can be seen as being either of a spiritual or multidimensional nature. Even more importantly, his most recent accounts appear to identify both the messengers and their message in great detail.

His first experience, when he saw the glowing orbs in the forest, where his son and some of his employees were present, is an example of several instances where his experiences were witnessed and confirmed by others. It is worth mentioning that since that first sighting, Bledsoe, his family, and many others who visited his property have witnessed anomalous phenomena there. They have seen orbs of various sizes, some of them the size of a baseball, others the size of a bus. All of them were glowing, they were often diamond shaped, and they appeared to be both technological and somewhat intelligent.

On several occasions, the orbs have had physical effects on the bodies of the experiencers, possibly through some kind of radiation. For example, when Bledsoe tried to take a photo of the orbs, the memory card in his camera melted. This, naturally, might raise questions about the veracity of the experiences from a strictly materialistic point of view.

How can we prove the truthfulness of an experience without physical evidence? This is a question all experiencers of anomalous phenomena face on a regular basis. Does the acknowledgement of an anomalous phenomenon require a religious-type faith, or is it enough to acknowledge its possibility simply because many people experience it? For me, the second option is more convincing.

Among all the strange phenomena that Bledsoe continues to experience, I am most interested in his testimony from Easter 2012 when he claims to have had a visitation from a "White Lady" who had a message for him to share with the rest of humanity. According to his book and various interviews, on that night in 2012, his house was full of guests, mostly his children's friends sleeping over. Bledsoe says he woke up to the sound of a deep voice. He sat up on his bed, asked, "Who's there?" and checked his bedside clock. It was three a.m. In a trance-like state, he put his clothes on and, without any volition of his own, followed three shadowy, hooded beings who were about six feet tall. He left his house and walked with them in the direction of the wooded area nearby.

Then a series of strange events happened. First, he was handed a fluffy, puppy-like object which felt prickly in his hands. The object seemed to be a living creature but without legs or a head. Bledsoe was told by the hooded apparitions that the fluffy object represented humanity in its current state of development—directionless. Still in a trance, Bledsoe put the "puppy" into his dog kennel. Suddenly, he felt a strong wind and saw a translucent bull galloping towards him, which disappeared just as quickly as it had appeared.

Only then, after the frightening experience with the bull, did Bledsoe see a beautiful white lady hovering about six feet above the ground. She was four to four-and-a-half feet tall and wearing a white dress with saggy sleeves and had translucent hair. She said to him, "You know why I'm here. You must tell what you've experienced."

Since Bledsoe was wary of sharing his experiences after the public ridicule he had experienced in the past, she reassured him that from now on, she would help him with evidence. She also told him there was a power shift in Heaven that had something to do with the return of the divine feminine. The following morning, he was found lying unconscious by the back door of his house.

The next sighting of the White Lady happened a year later, also during an Easter weekend, in 2013. Bledsoe was awake in his bed when a beautiful light levitated him above his bed then through the roof of his house. He found himself in a clear ball that took him to a place in a desert, which he thinks was somewhere in Utah or a place with similar landscapes. There, he saw the White Lady for a second time. He did not remember what she told him, except that when the alignment of the star Regulus would appear in the gaze of the Sphinx, a new knowledge would be born unto humanity.

Apparently, Bledsoe's publisher had the information checked. That particular event—Regulus becoming aligned with the Egyptian Sphinx—will take place in 2026.

The Lady of Fatima

The sightings of a lady or a white lady in the sky under anomalous circumstances are traditionally equated with sightings of the Virgin Mary by Catholics or with UFO sightings by the UFO community. Depending on what source we want to rely upon, there have been 363 apparitions of the Virgin Mary in totality through recorded history while other sources claim that there have been at least 400 apparitions in the 20th century alone. Whichever number is correct, these phenomena are not rare—and for that reason, they are worthy of investigation.

Very few of these incidents have been acknowledged by the Vatican. One that has been approved by the Vatican as legitimate and is also the most discussed in UFO circles is the sighting in Fatima, Portugal. The Virgin Mary—or White Lady, if we remove the Catholic connotation—is said to have appeared six times to three children between 1916 and 1917. These sightings became so widely spoken of that, at one point, 70,000 people showed up at Fatima, where they witnessed a "miraculous solar phenomenon in which the sun appeared to fall towards the Earth," as described in the *Encyclopedia Britannica*. Other sources reported that the sun kept changing colors from white to yellow to blue, as well as alternating its shape and spinning every seven to ten minutes (Leviton 2005).

The unusual "solar phenomenon" is probably the reason this particular event is widely discussed in UFO circles. Did spectators really see a woman surrounded by light, or could it have been a series of lights in the sky often identified by researchers as UFOs? As is frequently the case with UFO sightings, different witnesses observed divergent phenomena, but most of them experienced something they considered both unusual and life changing.

The Fatima Secret (Whitley Strieber's Hidden Agendas) by Michael Hesemann, published in 2008, gives comprehensive descriptions of several events that the children and later the large crowd experienced. The main value of this book lies in its detailed history of the apparitions in Fatima that predated the White Lady's appearance. However, it is important to remember that the book was written by a Vatican journalist and focuses on the strong religious themes as they were experienced by the three children (Jacinta, Lucia, and Francisco). In *The Fatima Secret*, the children were convinced they had seen the Virgin Mary and that her visitation had happened when they were praying, specifically by saying the rosary.

According to the children's testimonies, as collected by Hesemann, the first unusual sighting took place when they were praying while watching a herd of sheep in the hills near Fatima. They looked up and, above the treetops, saw a boy about fourteen or fifteen years old who was whiter than snow. They interpreted him as an angel of peace, asking them to pray with him. When the children came back to the spot the next day, the magic was still in the air, as if the apparition had opened a door to another dimension. The children encountered the angelic boy at least two more times before on May 13 when the White Lady showed herself for the first time.

The children said this apparition greeted them with the same words that many angelic visitors for centuries are said to have used when confronting astounded humans: "Don't be afraid, I won't hurt you." She told the children she was from Heaven and that they should come to see her on the 13th day of every month.

Hesemann goes into detail about exactly how the Lady appeared to the three children in the same manner for each sighting. First, they spotted the Lady floating above an oak tree, dressed completely in white, brighter than the sun, with rays of light around her. She was less than five feet away and the children were embraced by her circle of light. The physical depiction of the Lady in Hesemann's book is as follows: She was about four feet tall and had dark eyes. Her head was hooded. When she opened her hands, a bright light shot out at the children. A similar encounter with a young woman of the same description happened to one of John Mack's abductees in his book *Abduction: Human Encounters with Aliens* (1994), but with erotic overtones. I will discuss this later in this chapter.

A valuable aspect of Hesemann's book is that he has compiled many testimonies from the big event that took place on October 13, 1917. The White Lady had promised a miracle on this date. Hesemann's is the most detailed account I can find, but I have one warning: You need to be patient enough to move through the author's devotional Catholic descriptions of the events as depicted by the three children.

As news spread that a miracle would happen, the children's parents were suitably alarmed by the situation and tried to elicit a confession out of their children, believing they had made up the whole story. Even the local priest begged the children to admit they were deluded or had made up the story, but they persisted with their belief that something would happen.

The Fatima crowds gathered on the day of the next event, even though there was torrential rain. Sometime around one o'clock in the afternoon, the rain stopped, and Lucia told the crowd that the Lady was coming. The 70,000 eyewitnesses described different phenomena, ranging from the sun rotating and changing colors to rotating like a huge wheel of fire. Someone noted that people were able to look at the sun without being blinded and that the sun suddenly started dancing and looked as if it was tearing itself away from heavens, while at the same time it was throwing out beams of light in various directions, covering everything in different colors. Another testimony says the sun had a clearly defined outline and rushed down at the observers, then started rotating like a ball of fire at a dazzling speed.

The children experienced the same series of events they had during previous visitations of the White Lady. Only the children saw the White Lady, and others reported that their faces were transformed by wonder.

I must give some credit to Hesemann's open-mindedness, because although it is apparent he believes in the religious nature of the apparitions, he also observes that some writers have suggested these apparitions were holographic images projected by alien intelligence. He adds that people who have had UFO experiences often find themselves spiritually transformed and some even develop healing abilities. This seemed a stark remark from a Catholic Vatican journalist until I found out that he was well known in Germany for his books on UFOs and only later in his career had turned to topics associated with Catholicism.

Whitley Strieber, who is listed as Hesemann's editor, wrote the introduction to the English-language edition of *The Fatima Secret*. Strieber is the author of *Communion* (1987), a famous book about his personal experience with alien encounters, as well as several other books on anomalous phenomena that followed.

Apart from the testimonies of the children, both Hesemann and Strieber focus on the "three secrets" that the White Lady apparently revealed to the children: The first one was a vision of hell; the second one the prediction of the end of WWI and the warning that if humanity does not correct its ways, another great war would take place; and the third one warned of the persecution of Christians in the 20th century. The third prediction, however, is much discussed as it is believed that the Vatican revealed only a part of that message. Some even argue that there is the fourth message which was not shared yet with the public.

In addition to Hesemann's book, I have found two interesting descriptions at *Ignatium Today* (May 2024), a website for young Catholics. They are interesting because they include two testimonies originally published in an "anti-Catholic" newspaper from Lisbon called *O Seculo*. The testimonials came from two atheists who were both present at the October 1917 sighting: Avelino de Almeida, the editor-in-chief of *O Seculo* at the time, and Dr. Jose Maria de Almeida Garrett, a professor at the Faculty of Sciences at the University of Coimbra. Their testimonies ridicule the "dumbfounded peasants" who showed the typical expression of the superstitious in believing they had observed a biblical miracle.

However, although both men denied the religious aspect of the phenomena, they also experienced a set of unusual events. Almeida wrote that the sun trembled and made strange and abrupt movements that were outside of all cosmic laws. He said he saw the sun dance. Dr. Garrett observed that there were also changes of color in the atmosphere. Looking at the sun, he noticed that everything was darkening. He looked first at the nearest objects and then extended his view further afield as far as the horizon. Everything he saw had assumed an amethyst color—not only the objects around him but the sky and the atmosphere itself. Then everything both near and far shifted again, taking on the color of "old yellow damask."

Yet another take on the events of October 1917 in Fatima is given in a May 2024 episode of Whitley Strieber's *Dreamland* podcast entitled "The First and Greatest UFO Event in the 20th Century and Whitley under Pressure." In it, Strieber interviews Francisco Mourao Correa, a Portuguese researcher specializing in the Fatima events.

In this interview, Correa makes a few interesting statements about what had happened in Fatima. His accounts are free of the Catholic connotations of Hesemann's book. According to Correa's sources, the children did not originally refer to the Lady as the Virgin Mary, and not even as the Lady, but rather said that they had seen a female-shaped apparition. A thunder-like sound was heard, and then the female-shaped being appeared, covered in bright light.

Correa claims that people around the children, trying to explain the phenomenon within their own system of beliefs, decided that it must have been the Virgin Mary. In fact, Correa believes it was Jacinta's father who concluded that the apparition had to be the Virgin, because Jacinta told him it had come from Heaven. This was probably the reason later descriptions became increasingly Catholic-oriented; that is, the White Lady started to look more like the Virgin Mary in a golden dress with a rosary in her hand. An artistic representation of the female-shaped apparition as the Virgin Mary was not created until the 1920s; when one of the three children, Lucia, saw it, she insisted that it did not represent what she had seen during 1916-17 events.

Correa also makes this interesting point: At least two separate groups of psychics, one in Lisbon on February 7 and another in Porto on May 11, had received a message that something extraordinary that would impact the whole of humanity would happen on May 13, 1917. Correa asserts there is a paper trail confirming this claim, as both of the psychic groups paid for an advertisement in their local newspapers saying that something of great significance would occur on May 13, which was the date of the first sighting in Fatima.

In the same interview, Correa gives additional descriptions for the phenomena through testimonies not included in Hesemann's book or in *O Seculo*. These include balls of fire, flying hats, disk-shaped objects, and silvery disks with flashing light coming from behind the clouds accompanied by great thunder, which later dissolved to buzzing sounds. Correa thinks the reason people believed they saw the sun dancing in the sky was because the flying orbs exuded heat that dried their clothes, which had previously been soaked by the torrential rain earlier that day. The few cars parked in the vicinity were damaged by the heat of the flying orbs, and some of their gasoline tanks exploded during the event. The witnesses, Correa says, had no other point of reference on how to explain what they had observed, so they attributed it to the zigzagging sun.

Correa also claims something that was not mentioned in other testimonies: there were people who did not experience anything at all. This is particularly strange, as others observed the flying objects even though they were twenty kilometers (12.4 miles) away from the actual location of the event. The fact that some of the people gathered during the event did not witness anything at all suggests that in what happened in Fatima, and quite possibly in other instances of phenomena of this kind, whether anything was actually seen depended on the level of openness those people had to the possibility of the unusual occurrence.

At the same time, some of the observers believed they saw three human-like figures inside one of the flying orbs/suns. This was the most interesting part of the conversation for me, as it confirms yet again how our mindsets influence our interpretations of any usual event. Both Strieber and Correa find it amusing that the observers who saw the three human-like figures believed they must have been the Christian Holy Trinity, because this interpretation agreed with the observers' religious beliefs. However, neither Strieber nor Correa question their own belief, which is that the phenomena witnessed in Fatima had to be part of a UFO event of extraterrestrial origin.

While researching the sighting, I was surprised at how difficult it was to find objective sources of information. It almost felt as if it has been left there for our imagination—or perhaps as if no one with scholarly authority wants to touch it. All the academic papers I have consulted fall into three categories: 1) those written by devout Catholics who have no doubt that what happened in Fatima was a miraculous apparition of the Virgin Mary asking people to repent their sins; 2) works by scientists who want to ridicule the whole event and some important aspects of what was reported; and 3) papers by UFO enthusiasts who come with their own assumptions. The only academic paper I have found helpful, which attempts objectivity, is "Fatima pictures and testimonials: in depth analysis" (2021) by Phillipe Dalleur.

Dalleur uses a complex mathematical analysis of photographs of the event from October 1917. He concludes that the event was not of a meteorological, psychological, or physiological nature. In simple words, it was not a psychosis the crowd experienced, and it was not just a weird weather event. Dalleur says that the photographs clearly show two main light sources of similar brightness in the sky casting faint shadows, but neither of them was the actual sun, as some observers professed. He also acknowledges that the torrential rain before the event stopped abruptly once the two sources of light appeared in the sky. One other oddity observed right after the event was that the clothes of people present dried quickly, printing shadows visible as white parts bordered by dried areas. This suggests they were exposed to an infrared source of light normally not visible to the human eye.

Whether this is considered a religious or non-religious sighting might simply depend on the frame of reference: It can be viewed as an appearance of the White Lady, according to Bledsoe, or the Virgin, according to the Catholics, or a UFO, according to UFO enthusiasts Strieber and Correa. The event also can be seen as a multidimensional phenomenon. I put myself in the last category.

One way or another, something profound and out of the ordinary happened for most people present there. Under pressure from the local community in Fatima, the Vatican officially recognized the events in Fatima as a miracle in 1930. The position of the Vatican on other anomalous phenomena interpreted by some as visitations of the Virgin is that of *nihil obstat*—meaning "non-interference." In other words, people might choose to consider the phenomena as miracles and can choose to worship them, but the Church is wary of giving the events formal recognition.

The same reluctance of the Church to comment on anomalous phenomena remains. Although not specifically referring to the solar miracle of Fatima, the United States Conference of Catholic Bishops website from June 2024 says that the Vatican archives are full of stories of nuns witnessing orbs or other anomalous phenomena, but in the efforts to digitize the Vatican archives, these instances are not on their priority list. Another interesting pair of paragraphs from the website state:

> "While the staff at the Vatican archives acknowledge that their vast shelves contain accounts of miracles, they deny that any of their holdings pertain to aliens. The prefect wants to affirm that there is no document in the archives that regards extraterrestrial life," and scholars seeking such material at the Vatican should be "dissuaded from undertaking futile and unproductive attempts in this Apostolic Archive."[1]

Therefore, although many people experience Unidentified Anomalous Phenomena, no one seems to fully acknowledge them or explain their nature. However, we are going to delve deeper into the nature of the phenomena and ask the following question: Are these sightings of technological or spiritual nature?

UFOS AND THE OPENING OF THE UNSEEN DOOR

N ext, on our detective journey, I would like us to look into other possibilities for the space where the anomalous encounters take place. Sometimes these encounters seemed to be an interaction with advanced technology. At other times, they show similarity to spiritual experiences.

The first researcher to peek through the unseen door was Jacques Vallee. Vallee, who is referred to as computer scientist, venture capitalist, ufologist, and astronomer, was probably the first person to conceptualize UFO phenomena as interdimensional events. His interest in such exotic topics as UFOs and interdimensionality were taken seriously; this might have had to do with the fact he is a brilliant man with an excellent record as a scientist who devised a program for NASA to map Mars. For those familiar with the history of UFO research, Vallee also worked with Professor Allen Hynek on Project Blue Book, which was intended as a systematic study of UFO phenomena by the U.S. Air Force from 1942 to 1969. These are just a couple of ways Jacques Vallee made a name for himself.

For the purpose of our detective work here, it is his research on UFOs as interdimensional phenomena that intrigues me, so I read his book, *Passport to Magonia: From Folklore to Flying Saucers* (2014). The book was first published in 1969 and was considered heresy among UFO enthusiasts and skeptics. Both camps claimed that the compiled data was unreliable because the information was of a non-physical nature. A year or so later, the book became a classic in its genre.

Although Vallee is a scientist who believes that UFOs have a physical presence, he created *Passport to Magonia* as a catalogue of suspicious heavenly visitations from the most ancient to modern times. Reading *Passport to Magonia* feels like a familiar visit with an old friend, as Vallee's data has now been widely popularized through the Internet and popular TV shows. This impressive and well-written collection of historical and spiritual sources describes aerial phenomenon and, in some cases, simply anomalous experiences—throughout human history. If the book's content does not surprise anymore, it is because, for anyone interested in the topic, the information it contains has become a part of our popular culture.

His catalogue of sources goes back to 3000 BCE in Japan and through Ancient Roman, Medieval Europe, and the Mayan ruins of Palenque. Each location either shows carvings or shared chronicles of contact with a superior race that appeared to have a highly developed technology, often described in religious terms. One example is the Mayan engravings on a sarcophagus found in a pyramid in Palenque in southern Mexico. The engravings represent what is now termed the "Palenque astronaut"—a humanoid being sitting at the controls of some sophisticated machinery that looks like it might belong in a spaceship.

Another example is from late Medieval Europe, from the area of Tubingen in southern Germany. According to a chronicler, at exactly seven a.m. on December 5, 1577, great and strange clouds of unusual colors surrounded the sun. This in itself would not have been terribly unusual if the clouds had not been accompanied by loud sounds coming out of large, tall, white hats.

Whether these "hats" were similar to the luminous objects and orbs of light observed elsewhere is anyone's guess. However, the subsequent interpretation given to the people suggested this was an omen of an impending disaster, should humans not amend their ways. The same admonition was given when a third-century saint, St. Anthony, met an unusually small being on the deserts of Egypt. Here the saint's biographer used the incident to preach against heretics, early Christians living in nearby Alexandria who disagreed with the Roman dogma.

I do not think that we should dismiss the last two examples as completely fictional simply because they were used as a means of religious propaganda. They quite possibly are legitimate events describing what Vallee calls "aerial sailors from Magonia." These events fascinated the medieval people in Europe. Only later were they formulated as an opportunity to frighten people and force them into submission. They might indeed be reliable accounts of encounters with beings who seem to have visited us for centuries, if not millennia.

The next step in this investigation leads us a little bit further into the discussion of the nature of experiences associated with UFOs. Although I've had spiritual experiences all my life, I had never connected them with UFO phenomena until I read Diana Pasulka's *American Cosmic* (2019). I have always been curious about UFOs/UAPs and had no doubt that other intelligent life forms existed in the universe but had never thought of classically understood UFOs as actual spaceships. *American Cosmic* provided me with a new lexicon that has helped me to understand many liminal experiences I have had. Some of them could qualify as UFO related.

The premise of *American Cosmic* is that UFO experiences are very similar to religious experiences. For me, the book struck a chord, partially because she is a legitimate academic who considers this a valid topic for her book and also because Pasulka introduces readers to other high achieving individuals in the field of science who have experienced phenomena. In the beginning of her book, she clarifies that she is less interested in the "nuts and bolts" of the phenomena—that is, the spaceships themselves and alien technology—and more interested in the spiritual experiences that some people claim to have after their encounters with a UFO.

Many of the encounters described in *American Cosmic* don't involve spaceships but rather more ephemeral objects or entities that often present themselves as orbs and less-physical forms. Indeed, some of the experiences are closer to what are traditionally considered spiritual phenomena, which takes Pasulka to an exploration of how our consciousness can communicate with non-human intelligences.

The example from the book that stands out for me is described by an experiencer whose wife's beloved dog had become paralyzed. When his wife began praying to God and angels to cure her dog, she saw an object floating above the ground that was probing her with its lights. As a Catholic, she interpreted the event as a visitation from angels. However, her husband described it as a plasma object or plasma being. Since the dog was miraculously cured, two possible interpretations come to mind. From a religious viewpoint, what they had witnessed was a healing occurring after an angelic visitation. From a scientific point of view, the plasma orbs could have been a form of technology unknown to us.

A very different testimony, which attempts to merge the spiritual and technological in *American Cosmic,* has to do with a person named Tyler D. and his protocols for connecting with non-human intelligences. In brief, Tyler D. is a scientist involved in several space programs who came up with revolutionary solutions to technical problems. Due to his connection with what he calls "off-planet intelligence," he has been extremely successful in the areas of space exploration and biomedical sciences. What is known about his methods is that, to increase his off-planet downloads, Tyler D. follows a number of protocols. These are very simple methods that somehow increase the conductivity of his connection with information that is normally not available to him. This information, he is convinced, comes from exposure to something that affects his thought processes through emitting higher-level energies and frequencies, which he believes are a part of a non-Earthly intelligence.

Should we take Tyler D.'s explanations at face value? They are *his* interpretations of *his* own protocols for getting in touch with higher-level intelligences. It is only natural for him to interpret his access to what he calls "the memory of scientific experiences" as coming via his mentors and his technological environment. By his own account, Tyler D. says that earlier in his career, an unnamed mentor told him new scientific breakthroughs would happen through interdisciplinary involvement between the studies of religion and mysticism. However, only a sentence later, he confesses it is his belief that this collaboration with mysticism will occur through the interface of mind and machine. To me, this is a nod towards Artificial Intelligence rather than spirituality.

Yet, Tyler D.'s story is compelling and, incidentally, familiar to every artist or mystic throughout history, with one exception: many of them would have described his off-planet connections as communication with the Source/God/Divine Intelligence, insight, or even inspiration. I believe all the above terms are correct and they describe the same experience but from different points of view. Our viewpoints are also affected by our mental states and intellectual or spiritual preferences. So, the off-planet intelligence for a scientist in a secret space program would be described as *insight* for a mystic or *inspiration* for an artist. This seems to answer the question as to whether UFOs/UAPs exist only materially as a form of empirical technology or whether they are also mental and spiritual phenomena.

What alarmed me about Tyler D.'s story was that, at the end of it, he seemed to make a surprising intimation that spirituality and technology might not be very different from each other and might potentially merge. Personally, I think that the blending of technological interpretations with spiritual contexts is potentially dangerous. It might be part of AI-focused agenda that wants us to forget our natural and intuitive connection with spiritual realms and equate them with technological downloads.

This is where I step away from the enthusiasm for technological prodigies, as they seem to measure spirituality with their engineering tools. I am more inclined to support Vallee's explorations of the other realities that occasionally open for us. If Magonia represents the opening of a space where humans and beings from celestial realms occasionally interface, then perhaps it is more real than we think.

DMT Experiences and Alien Worlds

At this point, I believe we need to probe deeper to determine whether it is possible that the space in which the events occur is neither purely spiritual nor technological. I would like to propose that, just as Vallee speculated, this space might arise from another dimension that is as real as ours—even though it might be very different from the reality we normally experience. If two realties could exist simultaneously, then under the right circumstances, a door or a break of a barrier between them could open for us. Would this mean that we could experience the other reality as well?

I can share an experience of that kind that might fall into the same category of an *interdimensional* encounter. The encounter took place several years ago. I was going through a difficult time. Ironically, after finishing my PhD and thinking my career would take off, I found myself temporarily unemployed and aimless, questioning my professional and creative choices.

One night while I was lying in bed, I saw two figures of light that appeared to be towering above me. They were light yellow in color and looked like elongated beings with abstract features. They looked tall and stretched out with lanky bodies and long, thin legs and arms.

My communication with them was not telepathic but rather through pictures and what looked like a combination of hieroglyphics and mathematical symbols. Even then, I knew that they were attempting to say something in a language that was too complex for me. They downloaded the information into my head, assuming that I would understand it, even though all I got from the message was, "It is important."

As I was considering the topic of a mythological third space where humans and other entities meet, I wondered whether there are specific conditions under which this space could open up for us. I found a book by a medical doctor, Slawek Wojtowicz Strassman, who explored these phenomena through his experiences with psychedelics. I was immediately interested. I have never tried psychedelics but have always been curious about their influence on our perception of reality and about the subsequent spiritual aftereffects, including the expansion of consciousness and connection to realities not usually accessible to us. Strassman, on the other hand, has plenty of experience with psychedelics and has written several books about this.

I read the first sentence of Strassman, Slawek Wojtowicz, Luis Eduardo Luna, and Ede Frecska's *Inner Paths to Outer Space: Journey to Alien Worlds through Psychedelics and Other Spiritual Technologies* (2008) and was hooked. It begins with an exploratory assumption that our consciousness is a mystery and that the association of our consciousness with matter is not as obvious as we would like to believe.

As a medical doctor interested in heightened states of consciousness and those periods when we perceive what is not normally available to us, Strassman explains situations that can lead to what I would call "spiritual events." Among them are changes to our physiology that are often used by people seeking a spiritual experience or a vision quest, such as fasting, sickness, fever, and the use of natural substances such as ayahuasca or other similar plant based hallucinogens.

These methods, especially the ingestion of psychedelic plants, were used by early humans—and apparently by some insects, including bees. They continue to be used in nature based religions by spiritual seekers of any tradition willing to explore alternative means of connecting with the Divine or presences from other realms. Strassman argues that these experiences of alternative realities and meeting distinct personalities point us in the direction of non-human intelligences contained within our consciousness.

Strassman describes a variety of experiences from volunteers whom he guides through the supervised intake of dosages of DMT. DMT (an acronym for Dimethyltryptamine) is found in many plants and was traditionally used for ritualistic, mind expanding purposes by shamans and, as some claim, the ecstatics of many traditional religions. Volunteers in Strassman's experiments experienced visual images of kaleidoscopic colors, bright light, and swirling energy often described by saints and advanced meditators. Many reported entering entirely different worlds or universes and planes of existence. Some of the participants perceived microscopic realities, such as the DNA helix, in the colors red and green. Others saw a flow of numerical data, which seemed completely conscious and purposeful, moving around at great speed.

The descriptions that caught my attention related to other planes of existence. For example, one volunteer found himself hovering over a planet, not very different from Earth. Another volunteer suddenly landed at a space station with many creatures, some humanoid and others android-like. In many of these interdimensional travels, the participants met beings who possessed consciousness, were very intelligent, and seemed generally more knowledgeable than humans.

On some occasions, the beings were surprised—and at times annoyed— that a participant had shown up in their reality. At other times, the beings seemed to be expecting them and offered guidance, insights, and predictions. One volunteer found himself in a high-tech nursery with a three-foot-tall being who was attending to him like a nurse when he heard other voices saying, "He has arrived."

This brings me to another important point that can help us to make a connection between anomalous experiences and UFOs. Strassman noticed that the descriptions from the volunteers in the guided DMT experiments had much in common with the alien-abduction narratives. The typical—if there is such thing—alien abduction consists of a meeting with humanoid beings, a bright light, and often a sense of paralysis. The abductees typically find themselves in some sort of laboratory, surrounded by strange symbols and receiving some unspecified treatment or physical or mental examinations, Strassman calls these procedures "neurological reprogramming."

For our detective journey, it is important to notice that in both the DMT experiments and reported alien abductions, the humans involved were taken to a sphere of being that mystics call beyond the veil. Ecstatics, mystics, and yogis often report traveling to other lands, not all of them friendly and not all of them beautiful, which might explain religious references to both Heaven and hell.

I love Strassman's distinction between physicality and "noncorporeality." The current, materialistic focus of science is interested primarily in physicality that can be measured and quantified. However, noncorporeality cannot be measured; it involves consciousness-to-consciousness contact, which is something our science at the moment cannot cope with and, sadly, dismisses as not worthy of scientific exploration.

Some of the volunteers in Strassman's experiments with DMT reported experiencing states of bliss and other features of what is commonly perceived as a "near death experience," such as movement through a tunnel, hearing music and voices, seeing a review of their lives, and being accompanied or guided by angelic beings. Like my own lucid dreaming experience, which I will recount later in this chapter, these participants felt that their experiences were more than real. Strassman concludes that mystical states include a change in our perception not only of space and time but also of the sense of who we really are. But in the case of Near Death Experiences, there is often an additional realization that we are connected to an unimaginably powerful creator—a belief shared by most religions.

Alien Abductions

The reason why I believe it is important to examine examples of these types of encounters is that, the more we acknowledge that they have happened to many people and that they occur more frequently than we would like to admit, the more we bring them to the light of our understanding.

Also, what I like about Mack's approach is that it gives us a systematic structure as to how the alien abductions happen. What I like even more about Mack's book is his focus on the spiritual or transformational dimensions of the abduction phenomena, because this is where my own interests lie as well. I think that this is also what Strassman appreciated about the work when he wrote about his patients' experiences taking DMT. The transformation of the perception of reality and the expansion of consciousness occurs in the aftermath of both DMT intake and abductions.

Mack's book *Abduction: Human Encounters with Aliens* (1994) is a classic now and it would be irresponsible of me in my detective work to omit it. Mack was a respected academic and psychiatrist from Harvard, and the publication of this book nearly got him fired because the topic was considered unworthy of scientific research by his rather narrow-minded colleagues.

Before I purchased the book, I listened to several interviews with him, and he struck me as both a serious researcher and a caring, honest man who simply wanted to investigate a phenomenon that very few have dared to touch, due to the stigma associated with it. I was surprised that I could not find *Abduction* either in the University of Queensland Library, which is one of the biggest universities in Australia, nor in the Queensland State Library. Since I buy many books, to save money, I often purchase the Kindle versions—but *Abduction* was not available on Kindle, either. I eventually managed to find the paperback for sale online. But it's strange that a classic book like this one, written by a Harvard chair of Psychiatry, was so difficult to obtain by normal means. This somehow fits in with Mack's history after he wrote the book.

Upon the publication of *Abduction* in 1994, the Dean of Harvard Medical School appointed a committee to investigate Mack, as the dean believed that conducting research on alien encounters was professionally irresponsible. In short, Mack had written about something that was either considered a terrible taboo by other psychiatrists or, worse, he had entered the territory of alien abductions a little too early—before the public had been *allowed* to speak about it in any serious way.

Even now, at a time when legitimate academics are allowed to research this subject, in hindsight, the school's attitude seems somewhat bizarre. Fortunately, with the help of Daniel Sheehan, an accomplished Constitutional solicitor who is also interested in extraterrestrial matters, Professor Mack was allowed to continue with his work. It seems to me—and this is only my own reflection—that people who are allowed to write and speak about aliens are handpicked by someone and therefore permitted to do this kind of research, while others who do this kind of work without that permission are persecuted.

When Mack's *Abduction* arrived, I read the whole 400-plus pages of it in a day. And for the life of me, I could not figure out why Mack had suffered persecution from his own colleagues during his lifetime. The book is a well written, well researched account of some of his patients' memories, recovered during the process of hypnosis, about what they believed to be alien abductions. Mack does not point fingers at anyone, is not a threat to anyone, and is not conspiratorial in any way. He simply writes that some of his patients believed they had been abducted by aliens, and he collects and compares their testimonies with each other—something that any field researcher would do.

But before we can delve deeper into the transformational aspects of abductions, it is useful to focus on the similarities of the abduction phenomena in Mack's book. Mack therapeutically regressed sixty-seven people who claimed to have been abducted, which is a considerable number.

Out of that group, only thirteen are discussed in his book: eight men and five women. Most of the abductions happened in the experiencers' bedrooms, while they were driving, or, less often, when they were walking in nature. The abductions usually happened at night or in the early morning hours. Although the abductees had some memory of the events, it was primarily during hypnosis that those details were revealed. Some also realized that their abductions had started to take place at a very early age.

The beings the abductees met were most often colored a classical gray with short, dispassionate, large eyes and tiny lips. In some cases, they were reptile-like or insect-like, or they were beings of light. So there was some variety there: some, like grays, appeared to be more robotic than others.

These are the characteristics marking the typical early abduction scenario, based on Mack's research: It is night, and a child notices strange little beings with small lips and big eyes. The beings may be frightening to the child or, on more rare occasions, they are trying to play with the child. The experiences of abduction seem to become more frightening and unpleasant from adolescence through to adulthood. In some cases, the abductee experiences floating from their bed through the walls of their room and through the roof of the house to a spaceship, against their will.

Although this kind of experience would be unnerving even to the bravest among us, the most apparent reason the abductees are terrified is that the whole process happens without their consent. Some of the experiencers feel a deep fury and resistance to what is happening—and we can easily understand that. They then find themselves inside some sort of spaceship, and the recollections here are eerily alike: There is a constant humming noise, as in Wolski's case, and some kind of control console on the ship. Most described the presence of a taller leader who gives instructions to the grays.

Apart from the abductees being floated out of their bedrooms or cars without their permission, the other disturbing elements of the abductions are the medical examinations, performed with unfamiliar mechanical instruments. These examinations are often focused on penetrating their sexual organs, sometimes also their head, and less often their chest. Many experiencers also feel that the aliens communicate telepathically with them and can, literally, read their minds or get into their heads with their thoughts.

Upon waking, the experiencers remember only bits and pieces of what has happened. Their recollections feel like strange, disturbing, lucid dreams—but which seem very real and different from other dreams that one might experience. It is almost as if these people have been pulled into a different reality that does not necessarily fulfill all the criteria of complete physicality, but which is also more material or real than a dream.

In my own research into spirituality and in Strassman's research with DMT, these experiences touch upon something that is similar to what mystics of all traditions experience. It also allows for the idea that the experiencers have entered another realm.

Abduction or Lucid Dreaming: Two Personal Accounts

Interestingly, I can share two accounts with elements of abduction similar to those mentioned by John Mack in *Abduction*. One is my experience, which was benevolent and could also be interpreted as a strange, lucid dream. The second account belongs to a woman who related her experience to me.

A few years ago in Mount Martha, Victoria, Australia, I woke up at night and checked the clock. It was only 2.30 a.m. I had a sense that I had awakened in the middle of something and needed to go back to finish it, so I fell back to sleep. There I returned to what seemed to be a medical examination in a white room. I could not see much, as the edges of the room were blurred. But something felt off and I thought that someone was trying to deceive me. I did not feel threatened or scared in any way, but I had a feeling that the people in the room—the "doctors"—were hiding their true identities as well as the true purpose of the examination. I found myself half reclining on a seat that appeared similar to a dentist's chair.

At the very moment I thought that I was somehow being deceived by the doctors, one of them turned around to face me. He was charming and telepathically informed me that I was definitely not being deceived. His communication felt insincere. To make it even more suspicious, the doctors all looked exactly the same, as if they were clones of each other or holograms of the same man. Sensing my uneasiness, the doctor reassured me again that all was indeed normal. I detected a concern in him that he had been found out. My mind became even more lucid, as if I were coming out of the state of being drugged.

Another thought entered my mind, "Ah, they've fooled me because they can get into my mind."

Once I had this thought the man turned to face me again and I heard telepathically, *She knows! Time to stop.* I woke up feeling pleased with myself that they did not manage to deceive me for too long. I looked at the clock—it was still 2:30 a.m. I thought, *How is it possible that I was with the doctors and it is still 2:30?* Only then did it strike me how strange the whole thing was and that something very real, but somehow completely amiss, had happened.

I think it is worthwhile sharing the experience of a woman—let's call her Bryn—who recently listened to my testimony about my experience with the "doctors" on a podcast about UFOs and anomalous phenomena. She did not want to talk about it publicly but agreed that I include her description in this book under a different name. This woman is part of a broader circle of my friends who had previously never spoken about this. Bryn chose to describe one of her five abduction experiences.

Bryn had contacted me a few days after the release of the podcast, saying she had had similar experiences to mine. She noted the five main points of similarity between her recollections and mine: 1) They took place in a laboratory environment where some beings pretending to be human were in control; 2) There was a sense of being taken rather than participating voluntarily; 3) The events took place out of three-dimensional space-time, which created a time loss; 4) We experienced an inability to move while being in the laboratory, as if we were under anesthesia; and 5) The missions were aborted as soon as she regained her consciousness.

Despite the similarities between our experiences, her description contains many more details. At the time of the experience, which she called an abduction, she was sharing a hotel room with her mother. As Bryn was drifting off into sleep, alien beings placed her on something that resembled a table. There were green rods on either side of her, and she was gripping the rods. The beings were adamant that she had to grip the green, glowing rods. She tried with all of her might to fight the anesthesia, something she had never done before during these experiences, and attempted to open her hands and spread them wide to get them off of the rods. Her defiance created a commotion among the beings, and she started to return to consciousness, both in the operating room as well as in the hotel room.

Bryn described feeling as if she were dipping down to the hotel room and then coming up to the laboratory and then moving up and down between the two realities. She knew this feeling had to do with her refusing to hold on to the green, glowing rods. The beings soon realized that this time they had been unsuccessful with her, and as such, they aborted the mission. When Bryn opened her eyes, she saw her mother was in the exact same position on her bed, still awake, unaware of anything that had happened to her daughter. Whatever had happened to Bryn was not perceivable to other people in the three-dimensional field of experience, as she described it.

Whether these two accounts relate more to the abduction testimonies or lucid dreaming, I really do not know. What I am certain of is that they happened somewhere where these two possibilities could exist concurrently.

Whatever the alien worlds are, it appears that we can access them in states of consciousness different from our usual fields of perception. As we have already investigated, the space in which they occur is sometimes called *liminal,* that is, between two parallel realities. Yet, a more precise explanation of that space is possible and that is why we will look at the work of Professor Jeffrey Kripal.

THE UNSEEN DOOR AS THE IMAGINAL

The references to Bryn's lucid dream or abduction experience remind me of the impressive research by Professor Jeffrey J. Kripal of Rice University in Texas and his book *Secret Body: Erotic and Esoteric Currents in the History of Religions* (2017). Kripal believes many academics are aware that things like UFOs and paranormal activities are real. He thinks they need to be discussed within the field of religion and spirituality. Fearing ridicule, not too many academics dare to speak out professionally. Fortunately for the purpose of our investigation into the spiritual aspects of UFOs, Kripal does talk about it and his work provides some useful insights.

I think it is extremely important that we start with the definition of *imaginal*, a word that Kripal repeats a lot. Coincidentally, Jacques Yves Leloup—the translator of and commentator on *The Gospel of Mary Magdalene*—also uses this word to mark out the space in which the spiritual vision of the author of the *Gospel* took place.

According to Kripal, the original coining of the term *imaginal* can be attributed to the 19th-century poet Frederic W.H. Myers, who referred to "imaginal" as the moment of metamorphosis from larva to a butterfly—since, for the larva, a butterfly must appear alien. Indeed, not only Kripal but other spiritually oriented researchers of UFOs or the paranormal in general offer similar descriptions of the states in which these encounters and transformations happen.

In our investigative journey, the imaginal describes the space similar to lucid dreaming, just as my dream-not-a-dream was. The events in that space are both very real and completely absurd, such as "doctors" operating on me while appearing as both charming and deceitful, or two elongated figures of light trying to pass me an important bit of information that I could not understand, at least not on a conscious level.

For me, the most powerful testimony cited in Kripal's *Secret Body* is from Strieber Whitney, the author of *Communion* (1987), who related to Kripal that when he had asked the entities he encountered to show themselves in their true form, he saw a human being in another form. This led him to believe that we, as humans, are interdimensional beings, which is also my personal conviction. Kripal took this idea even further, concluding something that many esoteric traditions have taught us for centuries: that we are gods, but we are not ready to see it yet.

In this explanation, all alien appearances are the unexplored parts of ourselves trying to communicate with us. He calls this approach "secret humanism," while esoteric traditions have different names for it, including *gnosis* or *the Divine spark*—a secret to which we are entitled but one that institutional religions either do not know about or do not want to share with the rest of humanity.

If Pasulka says that she prefers to focus on the spiritual aspects of UFOs rather than the technological ones, such as UFO crash sites, Kripal openly admits that he is suspicious of the fear-based narratives of extraterrestrial invasions. He argues that this paranoid perception has been perpetuated mainly by two sources. One of them is the military intelligence and homeland security concerns about a possible alien invasion. The second one is fundamentalist religions, for whom everything mysterious has to be demonic or evil and needs to be destroyed. Both of these perceptions have been applied to interpretations of UFO sightings.

Kripal does a wonderful job of deconstructing a well-known testimony from June 24, 1947 by a man named Ken Arnold who reported seeing something silvery flying at incredible speeds in the mountains in Washington State. Considering the Cold War climate at that time, these sightings were immediately interpreted as flying saucers of suspicious origins. Apparently, Arnold was warned not to discuss his experiences publicly.

Somehow, the mysterious or even mystical aspect of UFOs was considered unspeakable, probably due to the preferred propaganda that this was evidence of a dangerous, technologically advanced species that was spying on us in a Cold War manner. What concerns me is that, in this fearful and paranoid narrative, the beauty and the miracle of connecting with another species of intelligent, and perhaps deeply spiritual, beings can be lost.

Indeed, later, Arnold's daughter admitted in an interview that there had been more to the description and that many important elements were omitted from her father's testimony, such as the apparitions above the mountains that were quivering with blue-white light in a rhythm similar to that of a beating heart. And, more to the point, her father was convinced that the apparitions were not mechanical at all. On the contrary, he believed they were life-forms of some sort.

I am convinced that this kind of phenomena occur in the imaginal space between dream and reality. And that this is precisely the unseen door to the miraculous worlds, whether we coin them alien or spiritual.

ANOMALOUS ENCOUNTERS AND THE MESSENGERS

Anomalous experiences, whether related to UFOs or not, are a part of our lives. They pierce through the veil of our physical reality and often astound us, yet they often remain a secret. The question is: Why do we keep these unusual experiences secret? Why did I keep my experiences secret?

On almost every occasion, it seems that I either *knew* I was not supposed to talk about my experiences, or I was told not to talk about them—but by whom? On the rare occasions when I shared an experience with people close to me, they quickly forgot about it after the initial "Wow!"—as if it had never happened.

I have had two of my own experiences with beings that could be classified as multidimensional encounters. I will share these two brief encounters and then proceed to the scientific and theological explanations of how they could be classified.

My first encounter happened when I was nineteen years old. I was sitting in my room in Lublin, Poland, and going through an intense experience of fear when I saw a presence that communicated with me telepathically, without words. The presence was pure, white light, of no particular shape; it was vaguely egg-shaped, but with fringes of light coming out of its sides. It looked like a portal or a large, vertical orb of some kind.

The presence calmly communicated to me that there was nothing to be afraid of. This telepathic transmission carried such peaceful energy with it that I began to relax my intense fear and started to feel profound peace. I left my room to tell my mom what had happened, but she just said, "That's good that you're more peaceful now," as if nothing unusual had happened.

The second experience occurred when I was living in Toronto with my first husband and was a few weeks pregnant. I had a lucid dream in which I saw my grandmother, who by then had been dead for fifteen years. We were both in a large, almost limitless room. It was nearly completely dark except that a light, almost like from a cinematic camera, shone on the precise spot where she was sitting on a chair. There was no other furniture there, just my grandmother on a single chair in a dark room.

"What are you doing here, *babcia*?" I asked. And she said, "I'm waiting for your baby." I woke up and learned that I had had a miscarriage.

These kinds of experiences are not easily understood, as they are not normal, and they are difficult to share. But they frequently imprint themselves on people in a very profound way, even if we choose not to return to them. The difficulty in deciphering such things lies at least partially in the fact that our understanding deepens as we evolve spiritually. What we might have thought or interpreted in our past about certain events can be very different from what we believe is true about them later. Also, there can be a considerable time lapse between any encoded communication during the contact and subsequent events in our lives that might bear them out.

What those in the religious sphere might consider angelic or demonic might nowadays also be seen as contact with good or bad aliens—depending on the quality of the subjects. Whether perceived as abductions or lucid dreams, the experiences seem to become considerably more positive and, in some cases, even beneficial once the experiencers drop their resistance and fear. The encounters connect the subjects with what I would call "multidimensional realities" that are well out of the scope of our regular sphere of experience. In other words, people were and are taken out of their comfort zone of known reality and into unknown realities.

But aren't we conditioned to our reality from childhood? Aren't our childhood visions disregarded as fantasies to meld our perceptions to a very limited understanding of what is possible for us?

Does the idea of multidimensional beings visiting us regularly—or even being an inherent part of our lives—go against what the UFO community believes? There has been an ongoing evolution of the name of that community to match what it encompasses: from Unidentified Flying Objects to Unidentified Aerial Phenomena to, most recently, Unidentified Anomalous Phenomena.

I believe the experiences I am discussing here are best described by the latter category. For me, this description signifies other intelligences attempting to communicate with us, primarily—but not only—through our consciousness, especially in the liminal spaces between our hardcore material reality and other possible states of being. These states have been experienced by people throughout the ages. This does not mean that these intelligences cannot communicate with us in a purely material realm or with technology, as is recounted in classic UFO phenomena that might include flying objects with beings inside.

Opening Our Minds to UAPs

What I have learned from my experiences is that to be able to see something, we first have to give ourselves permission to see it—or, even better, we need to allow for the possibility that something exists to be able to see it. Without this allowance, we cannot see. But first, we need to understand how our perceptions work and what can be considered real. Paul Brunton, in his book *The Hidden Teaching Beyond Yoga: The Path to Self-Realization and Philosophic Insight, Volume 1*, says a similar thing in a more systematic way.

I believe this is the part that relates closely to UFOs/UAPs and other anomalous experiences, especially to those cases when only some people perceive them, while others do not. First of all, Brunton begins his analysis with the statement that, "Any fact or event which is actually observed becomes entitled to the term experience." This is very encouraging for all people who have experienced UFOs/UAPs or any event out of the usual frame of perception. He assures us that observations of unusual phenomena should be given proper consideration.

Our mind requires three elements to be able to interpret or validate an unusual experience. The most important part, according to Brunton, is the association with past, similar experiences, since this allows us to categorize an experience based on our previous encounters with the same thing. If we have never had a similar experience in the past, we do not know how to interpret the new one and, consequently, we cannot understand it.

We can apply this approach to our line of inquiry. For example, when encountering an anomalous event—such as a UFO—for the first time, we are baffled. We often try to explain the experience in a way that makes sense to us, based on what is acceptable for us. If we are presented with a non-physical or highly unusual physical occurrence, we are likely to dismiss it, as it makes no sense to us because we have no memory of a similar occurrence. We might deny the event happened at all or we might convince ourselves that our mind or senses have played a trick on us. Either of these two explanations can give us peace of mind—but, at the same time, they discourage any further exploration as to what has actually happened.

The second most important thing for seeing is when we have an openness to new experiences, because then and only then we will attempt to decipher the unusual event and the meaning behind it. And only then will we not straightforwardly reject the event. For example, when we see or experience something new and unusual, we can attempt to understand it. All we need to do is to allow ourselves the smallest amount of curiosity. "Just a moment, what has just happened?" is a thought that can take us on a journey of mental exploration even if we have not had previous experience of a similar kind. And then we can determine whether that experience was real to us.

In this way, we admit it to our consciousness, to our personal bank of usual experiences. This, in turn, will help us to interpret other unusual new experiences, because we have previously mentally allowed ourselves to explore such things. I like to compare encountering UFOs/UAPs to going on an adventure; it must always involve an openness to the new. You cannot go on an adventure and expect that it will be the same as staying at home. I am not saying that we have to accept everything as real, but we need to be open to new experiences to be able to process them and assign a meaning to them.

This is precisely what the third and last element of Brunton's model gives us: We interpret what the experience means to us personally. By principle, this is a highly subjective exercise, because we perceive everything through the lens of our consciousness. The interpretation of each experience might differ from person to person, depending on how they process the three elements: Have they had similar experiences in the past? Were they open to the new experience, even if it did not fit into the normal range of perceptions? And, how had they explained it to themselves?

Brunton also addresses a point that I believe to be essential when discussing UFOs/UAPs: the objection of materially minded people to unusual occurrences. It is interesting, he says, that the people who most vehemently object to the reality of anomalous phenomena actually believe that these phenomena are possible—but only when they happen to great artists or saints. The greatest feats of creativity, for example, often happen in the imaginal spaces between sleep and waking or even when we are dreaming. We could also include into this category the intuitions of revolutionary scientists. However, these intuitions are deemed unreal when they happen to us.

Another, scientific rather than philosophical, attempt at explanation of unusual liminal experiences is explored by Professor Robert Epstein, an American psychologist and author. In his article, "Your brain is not a computer. It's a transducer," published in *Discovery Magazine* (2021), Epstein examines scientifically weird phenomena such as lucid dreams, near death experiences, and other events we habitually dismiss as not real—yet which everyone is aware of.

In nearly all of these occurrences, we encounter other entities, other realities, and other worlds in a very vivid way, sometimes more vivid than in our normal lives. These other intelligences not only communicate with us but, as Epstein believes, they also raise us to a higher level of consciousness. Epstein postulates that these realities are being "streamed" to us through something we colloquially explain as downloads. Epstein calls this the "neural transduction" theory.

What is significant about Epstein's theory is that he is convinced we can learn to simulate the anomalous events and therefore communicate more directly with the entities we encounter. In that way, we can control the streaming which, at the moment, seems to happen without our conscious volition. We could solve the mystery of the strange phenomena we experience but dismiss.

For our investigation, the most important thing about Epstein's research is that he does not deny the reality of anomalous phenomena. He only wants to be able to facilitate streaming in an objective, controlled way, which is how modern science operates.

Increasingly, I believe that our reality is much richer than we know. In fact, our reality expands as our field of perception expands. We know this is true with spiritual experiences: new realities open, and with them, new perceptual possibilities. And I think, on a purely intuitive basis, the strange times we are living in now are making the "doors of our perception" open just a little more. I, for one, find this liberating, if not challenging.

At the end, I agree with Brunton that more truth is needed, especially in these intense times. I would add that, to know more truth, we need to free ourselves from our habitual thinking about reality. Otherwise, if we continue explaining our experiences in strict material or technological terms, we might miss the most meaningful parts of our lives and the answers we are seeking as a species. Even worse, we might fail to understand messages from other realms that we need to hear. The truth, after all, might not be what we expect it to be, and the messenger might not be in the form we believed them to be.

UFOs, Angels, and Photons

If both the message and the messengers could be coming from outside of our normal realm of experiences, we need to ask ourselves: How it is possible for us to discern them and read their messages? Can modern science offer a possible explanation for the liminal space where these encounters happen?

This additional piece of the puzzle was solved when I found further explanation that made sense to me and gave me some clarity in an excellent book, *The Physics of Angels: Exploring the Realms Where Science and Spirit Meet* (1996) by Matthew Fox and Rupert Sheldrake. The book is written in the form of a dialogue between a theologian and Episcopal priest, Matthew Fox, and a scientist, Rupert Sheldrake. *The Physics of Angels* is an interesting read, filled with great insights. It marries spiritual and scientific perspectives with regard to the phenomenon of angels as messengers and UFOs.

The first thing that struck me in the book was the information that most narratives of encounters with angels start with angels saying the words, "Don't be afraid." That was also my first experience in my room in Lublin when I was younger, during an intense experience of fear. The second valuable thing that I learned from *The Physics of Angels* is Sheldrake's explanation of a new quantum physics which, in his opinion, has opened a door to a new cosmology. This new cosmology allows much more room for the ineffable, including such phenomena as angels. It becomes more and more apparent according to modern physics that our universe does not consist of matter, but rather of waves of creative energy expressed as light.

As the paradigm of science shifts from matter to energy, Sheldrake says, we have to admit that we know surprisingly little about the nature of the universe—and, I would add, our reality. We can no longer believe that there are set laws governing the universe, as Newton thought, since the laws of the universe seem to evolve proportionally to the progress of science. We live in an evolving universe which consists mostly of energy that is largely unknown to us.

Sheldrake then takes this thought even further, suggesting that this energy seems to be intelligent and present in everything, including the things once considered lacking in consciousness, such as planets, stars, animals, trees, and rocks. In a sense, this rehabilitates the old medieval concept that the planets have souls with their own personalities and vibrations and dance to the music of the spheres.

He makes also an interesting comparison between angels and photons. Photons, like angels, are non-localized; that is, they are where they need to be at any given time. They are also nonmaterial, as they have no mass and they move at the speed of light, like angels, which are described as being faster than thought. In a sense, photons behave like the angels of quantum physics.

Fox, the theologian, brings examples of the mystical visions of angels by Hildegard of Bingen, a 12th-century abbess from the Rhine Valley who astounded her peers with her wisdom, insights, and visions. There are very few examples of embodied, enlightened feminine figures accepted in institutionalized religions, and she was one of the greatest.

Hildegard learned from her visions that the entire universe was a "cosmic song" filled with the vibrations of angels, which are the intermediary between our Source and our physical lives. Angels want us to join in the universal connectivity and become "citizens of the Divine". They come to wake us up to this possibility and are connected to both below and above with love.

Based on Hildegard's ideas about angels, I would argue that angels have an intentional purpose in contacting us and therefore, these kinds of encounters are not random.

Not only do Fox and Sheldrake discuss the existence of beings we traditionally call angels, but they also consider the possibility of modern UFO phenomena being potentially angelic appearances. Their exchange concerning angels and UFOs is mostly theological as they elaborate on Hildegard of Bingen's writings about angels and how they appear to humans. For example, Hildegard insisted that humans do not see angels in their true form but rather in forms that are acceptable to us. This means they might assume the appearance of spiritual beings such as angels—or as technologically advanced beings such as aliens. Similarly, many modern-day experiencers of the UFO phenomena claim that they were told by aliens themselves that they had to change their appearance to satisfy the human sense of aesthetics. Otherwise, we would not hear their message.

The important takeaway from this discussion is that there are beings who want to connect with us and have a message to share. This is what matters for the purpose of this investigation. In the next chapter, we will investigate exactly who is trying to send us a message and what the message could possibly be.

ABDUCTIONS, THE FEMININE, AND THE EROTIC

If we agree that other beings, in different forms, want to connect with us, then this leads me to the most controversial aspect of UFO/UAP research: the even more sinister agenda in abductions where there is a sexual and reproductive element associated with genetic intrusion, either to alter us or to help the visitors.

Many people who claim to be alien abductees believe that their sexual organs have been regularly inspected and, in some cases, that women's eggs or men's sperm have been extracted without their permission for the sake of creating human-alien hybrids. Although this part of the abduction narrative does not feel very spiritual, we can pause for a moment and remember the stories of immaculate conception that are present in many religions— including the one I was brought up with, the Catholic tradition of the Virgin Mary—as examples. Perhaps an angel is an alien in disguise, or vice versa, depending on our system of beliefs.

The information on the virgin birth that resonates most with me is presented by Joseph Campbell in his book *Goddesses: Mysteries of the Feminine Divine* (2013), which is a collection of his essays and lectures on that topic. Campbell, a master of mythological analysis, writes that the virgin birth represents the birth of spiritual life in us and has nothing to do, mythologically or otherwise, with a biological anomaly. In this way, Campbell is taking a stance that the story of the virgin birth in all traditions has an esoteric and symbolic value, rather than being biologically possible. I would add that the concept of the virgin birth is a shift in human consciousness towards spirituality and multidimensional realities of ascension. It is a process of ascending consciousness within the human body.

There are, however, other opinions, which I will share here. Marguerite Rigoglioso, in at least three of her books—*The Cult of Divine Birth in Ancient Greece* (2011), *Virgin Mother Goddesses of Antiquity* (2010), and *The Mystery Tradition of Immaculate Conception* (2021)—believes otherwise. Through her research and intuitive downloads, she argues for the reality of immaculate conception, which she calls the evidence of Divine birth and parthenogenetic conception without male sperm. This form of conception, she argues, was practiced by ancient priestesses as a form of spiritual technology which allowed the priestesses to impregnate their eggs without any outside source.

Rigoglioso claims this was possible because they knew how to generate the necessary sexual heat within themselves to spontaneously create meiosis of their eggs. Both St. Anne and the Virgin Mary—Jesus' grandmother and mother, respectively—belonged to this tradition. In time, according to Rigoglioso, the process was degraded, and human women became impregnated—often without their volition—by interdimensional beings. Rigoglioso believes that this multidimensional intervention was a form of intrusion into processes that had originally been of a spiritual nature.

To simplify her line of thinking, the spiritual technologies used by ancient priestesses were somehow hijacked by interdimensional beings. One of the examples she gives is that of Olympias, the mother of Alexander the Great, who conceived during union with one of the personifications of the Greek god Zeus. I assume that the reason for this interference was to suit their own agenda, which was not necessarily serving humans in the best way. This is an interesting theory and although I have my own reservations about it, the part about intervention by multidimensional beings might help us to unpack some abduction stories in more detail.

Here we need to go back to two examples from John Mack's *Abductions*, as they are aligned with my own interest in the connection between sexual and spiritual. Some of the testimonies fit well with my own recollection with the "doctors." Even better, they also indicate that the alien beings contacted them to pass a message to humanity and used sexual means for this transmission.

In one chapter of Mack's *Abductions*, Ed, a technician in his early forties, recalls his abduction experiences when under hypnosis by Mack. Ed, like me, had an intense fear of doctors and hospitals. He also remembered some elements of his alien encounters before the hypnosis and was seeking more clarification. The initial regression took him to his early teens, as he wanted to uncover more details about his contact experience with aliens. The account I give here is a reconstruction of Ed's pre- and post-hypnosis story.

As a teenager, Ed and his friend traveled up the coast of Maine in July 1961. They camped in a car by the ocean. One night before they went to sleep, they were discussing how aroused they were and how they hoped they would meet some girls on the beach the next day. Suddenly, Ed saw two figures outside the car that were human-like but not exactly human. They had large, dark eyes. As I did in my doctors' dream, Ed sensed that these visitors were camouflaging who they really were. He felt a strange sensation at the bottom of his skull and his whole body started to float.

Despite knowing that all of this was happening without his permission, he was relaxed and happy as he was floated into a large, dome-like pod. The inside of the dome looked like an amphitheater with at least half a dozen beings. One of them appeared to be a "doctor" in charge who called the other beings, drones. All the beings—just as in my lucid dreaming experience— were gentle but somewhat deceptive.

Along with the doctor, Ed also saw a female figure: slim, having a triangular-shaped face with a largish forehead and with long, straight, thin, silvery-blond hair; immense, sensual dark eyes; and small lips and nose. He found her attractive, if unusual. She began filling his mind with sexual fantasies and when she sensed his resistance and distrust, she softly asked him not to fight the process. Ed had the strange sense that the figure was very familiar to him and was somehow connected to sinister memories from his childhood.

Eventually, Ed and the tiny blonde female being had intercourse that was very satisfying—but, at the same time, Ed knew that during the intercourse, the female was passing information into his mind. Ed sensed that, for her, the intercourse was a means of transferring information without his resistance. She then told him that they needed human sperm for their own needs, specifically to create special babies that would provide help to our planet and humanity alike.

She also told him that humanity was on a path of destruction and to change our ways we needed to "listen to the Earth." If we did not do this, the Earth itself would shake us off like bugs to get rid of us. The female figure also showed him how we had progressed from the playful creativity of nature to a destructive species that had done much damage and had now become the deluded hosts for malignant and distorted spirits, which the female entity and her associates were trying to ward off. Their goal was to bring both their race and humans back to a healthy symbiosis.

Several things fascinate me about this account. Yes, it could easily be dismissed as an adolescent sexual fantasy, but I am convinced it is much more. For example, I am puzzled by many similarities to other contact stories, including my own story: the floating, strange but pleasant feeling, even though what was going on was without our permission; the amphitheater with "doctors"; and the underlying sense of deception that the beings were hiding their true identities.

Another thing that intrigues me about Ed's story is the erotic aspect of it, specifically the use of sexual ecstasy by the alien blonde as a means of expanding Ed's consciousness to transfer important information. In my previous book, *The Other Goddess*, I explored the esoteric traditions that survive at the margins of most religions, the various methods of accessing the state of enlightenment or a connection with the Divine, including through sexual union between a woman and a man. These methods are revealed only to advanced initiates; I experienced them myself after my initiation.

The transmission of knowledge or messages through erotic means is not a new one. In the classical Tantric traditions of India and Tibet there exists a tradition of the *shaktis* in India or *dakinis* in both India and Tibet, which are disembodied female entities—or perhaps a better description would be female *energies*—which are often called upon before sexual practices of Tantra to help transmit energy and information exchange between the Cosmic Field of Consciousness and the couple engaged in a Tantric sexual union. In my case, this had nothing to do with any UFO experience but rather came about through study of esoteric texts and the formal initiation. All the same, there is one other similarity I can't ignore when analyzing my own anomalous experiences: the pod.

In fact, it is the pod that leads us to investigate the connection between UFOs and the messages they might have for us.

UFOS HAVE A MESSAGE

M any years ago, when I was a teenager in my room in Lublin, I distinctly remember asking about the purpose of my life. I was shown, either in a dreamlike vision or through memory, myself hanging somewhere in the Universe in what I would call a cocoon rather than a pod. Then I saw myself spending a lot of time in a space filled with books. The vision was a combination of a symbolic representation—what we nowadays call a download—and a dialogue or a negotiation.

The books or library were there to represent me studying but also signified access to knowledge and where I should seek that knowledge. Although I was alone in the cocoon, there were others—many of them, perhaps all of humanity or even all beings—hanging in their own cocoons among the stars. I understood that this was our place of origin to which we always return. Both the cocoon and the books and their symbolic value were downloads.

The third was negotiation on my side as I reached out mentally to the source of the download and asked that it would also honor my vital element and sense of adventure. Only then was I shown driving a car in the desert-like environment, the red soil with patches of grass as vegetation that represented the vast land of Australia to me. And only then did I accept this symbolic representation of my life's journey. In the vision, I was constantly moving between the elements: the cocoon, the books, Australia, and back again.

When I came out of this very vivid vision, I knew I had to write it down. I do not know whether it was the result of the vision or auto suggestion after the vision, but the last two parts of it have certainly come true. I have spent most of my life as a writer and an academic and therefore also in libraries and among books. And even though I had never planned to come to Australia, as I wanted to live in the North and South Americas, here I am.

The remaining question is, what was the cocoon about? For me, it was a place of origin, and I interpreted it in symbolic terms, while Ed interpreted his as an abduction—a physical experience. Is it possible that with at least some contact or abduction experiences, where we are taken to the place of our origin and meet again with our brothers and sisters, we are filled with fear because we normally do not remember where we have come from?

I believe that once we ask for the clarification of our life's mission and when we accept that mission, we can reach out again to the source of that information for support. In my mid-forties, while living out my purpose and having already been divorced twice, I purposefully reached out to that space once more, asking for a loving, male companion who would understand me—and I met my beautiful man.

In hindsight, the recollection of this experience, which is probably more common than most people would admit, teaches us that there is an intentional way of connecting with the imaginal space. This, in turn, means that our communication with the nucleus of that space might be mutual. I believe that the analysis of experience clarified for me the subtle difference between the liminal and imaginal space and refined my definitions of them. *Liminal* is a space between realities or dimensions that, under some conditions, opens for us. *Imaginal*, however, is an opening in our consciousness that connects us with our original Source and facilitates a line of communication and even co-creative engagement with it. As far as I know, the only way of being certain whether the experience takes place in the liminal or in imaginal space is whether we can freely access it and actively participate in it.

The last and perhaps most important aspect of Ed's experience was the actual message that the female figure passed to him: the healing of human collective consciousness and both the urgency and significance of that collective healing for the sake of the Earth and the entire universe. I have always found it puzzling that a message of such importance was only remembered after a period of time had passed or after the intervention of hypnosis. In many experiences of such events, the experiencer remembers the encounter itself and that they were told something important, but they cannot recall the content of that message. It appears the memory of the message is to reveal itself when the experiencers, or perhaps all of humanity, are ready. We are slowly awakening, but clearly not quickly enough, as so much is still unknown.

The sense of mission on a much larger scale is present in Eva's testimony in another chapter of Mack's *Abductions*. Eva was thirty-three years old when she contacted Mack regarding her dreams and memories of contact with extraterrestrials. I have chosen Eva's testimonies because in the book, it is clear she considers herself to be a spiritual person and, like many others who claim to have been in contact with other beings, she has also had other anomalous experiences unrelated to the abductions, as well as persistent nightmares.

Eva's first abduction experience happened at about the age of four when she saw three small beings in her bedroom examining her genitalia. The experience was not erotic, not only because of her age, but also because the little beings were examining and probing her but used no force and showed no sexual arousal. This was scientific exploration for them, and she was their specimen.

Based on her experiences, Eva observed that ETs have the ability to enter our space and dimension or leave it at any time they want. Just as Hildegard of Bingen described angels eight centuries earlier, Eva says the aliens we physically see take on this form when they enter our dimension. In their own dimension, they do not exist in the same form. Like me, she believes they are real and exist in a place or dimension where reality is not physical. She says she is also convinced that all abductees have their own separate missions and that abductions themselves are a means of removing mental obstacles that deplete our connection with Source.

She assures us that, although abductions have a spiritual meaning, they are also physically real. Like other abductees, she found her experiences initially terrifying, but she believes that, once we stop being fearful of the process, we gain access to vast fields of information that the beings make available for us. Interestingly, she believes that we should not waste our energy on trying to prove the existence of aliens or the mechanical aspects of this. Instead, she feels we need to focus on the messages they give us, such as changing our ways that are leading to the destruction of our planet, including the destruction of the natural environment. It is a mistake to consider these phenomena in solely materialistic/mechanistic ways.

Anyone who had either a profound spiritual awakening or a significant anomalous encounter knows how these experiences change us. Sometimes the change is sudden, and other times it is gradual. Often, the change is not welcomed, or at least not in the form in which it appears. Our lives get rewired. People, jobs, and friends are removed as if they are inconsequential byproducts of what now seems to be our old life. The new life has not presented itself to us yet and is probably not the life that we dreamed for ourselves, and we are left in a vacuum of uncertainty.

For some people, this experience also had erotic undertones. Should it come as a surprise that an erotic act, which can carry an immense energy and intensity, might act as a powerful gate to other worlds?

This might explain why some of the encounters were traumatic for experiencers. It might also help us to understand that even the accounts of ecstatic saints were often woven with fear as much as with awe. The well-known religious figure St. Teresa of Avila—a 16th-century Spanish mystic—did not like to talk about her ecstasies, but a superior asked her to write a record of them. What we read about her spiritual ecstasies is not what I had imagined as a young Catholic. I thought ecstasies were pleasant and well ... ecstatic, as envisioned by Bernini's sculpture, "The Ecstasy of St. Teresa." But one translation by E. Allison Peers of St. Teresa's writings paints a different picture.

> "Indeed, I confess that in me it created great fear—at first a terrible fear. One sees one's body lifted up from the ground—and although the spirit draws it after itself—and if no resistance is offered does so very gently, one does not lose consciousness—at least, I myself have had sufficient to enable me to realize that I was being lifted up."[2]

Does this remind us of anything? In particular, John Mack's volunteers described almost identical experiences and, also, said that their experiences of being floated to the "amphitheater" of a spaceship were much more pleasant when they let go of fear. Only then were they also able to absorb important messages regarding the good of our planet.

There are many narratives of spiritual transformation that include both an unusual event and an abrupt change in our beliefs. Another well-known example comes from the Bible in Acts 9 where the Apostle Paul is struck by white light on the way to Damascus. Although within the context of Christianity, Paul's experience is explained as a conversion to Jesus' teaching, it also reflects a larger, symbolic representation of dramatic transformation that is often drastic in nature, a change from the old to a new self.

To summarize this part of our detective work: In principle, I have nothing against the existence of highly evolved entities, whether technologically advanced or spiritual. In fact, I personally believe that such entities do exist, as I have had some experiences with them when the unseen door to imaginal spaces opens enough for me to perceive them. If I listen to my intuition, it tells me that both worlds exist, each with its own unique voice. We must decide to which voice and what message we will listen to and what subsequent action we will take.

Some of the beings that people have encountered appeared to be at least partially of mechanical nature, while others were what traditionally would be called angels or beings of light. Both carry a message for us and are eager to share information with us, whether of technological or spiritual kind. At times, the beings act as if they are concerned about the future of our species and our planet and wish to influence the direction we will choose to take.

Above all, I would like to point to the obvious but often overlooked or dismissed notion that when the alien goddess-like presence appears— whether the White Lady, the Lady of Fatima, or the seductive alien female of one of Mack's abductees—she often seems to bring a message of peace and spiritual transformation. Is it too much to ask whether this is our suppressed feminine form of a larger field of consciousness reaching out to us through the liminal or anomalous? Perhaps what we call the liminal or anomalous is the seat of that form of consciousness we so desperately need now.

We live in an era when fascination with materialistic determinism in science and attempts to use AI technology to give us mechanical "immortality" have taken us to the very dangerous end of the technologically focused mind. This kind of intelligence is based on logic and calculation alone, at the expense of the deeper wisdom cherished by the goddess traditions of the past, which tell us a different story and teach us different possibilities that can await us.

Perhaps we could open to the possibility that both our reality and the entire universe are pulsing with life. Whether we see it or not, consciousness is the very stuff from which everything is made, including all physical existence—not the other way around. Consciousness, or some Divine Spark, chose millennia ago to manifest itself in physical forms. Eventually, all physical forms, including us, will flow back to their point of Origin.

In later parts of the book, we will look at the Gnostic writings about Mary Magdalene and the other sacred stories preserved in the goddess tradition texts, including Inanna, Demeter, and Sophia. They are the guiding lights in the quest to perceive a broader, more open, more alive, and more compassionate universe.

But first we need to explore what might await us if we continue to ignore these messengers and the messages we receive.

Let's enter together that hypnotic, imaginal space where all visions and miraculous encounters happen. In that space, I am as I am in this moment: sitting in my garden with my dog at my feet. It is a sunny autumn day, and after the tropical rains, the eucalyptus trees and leaves of the palm trees around the house are intensely green. The colorful red and blue parrots hang flirtatiously from the branches of the bottle brush tree. The black-and-white butcher birds and the small brown birds with yellow beaks sing joyfully. Yes, this is how I am now, and this is how I enter the space of the imaginal—the liminal space between the "real" and the "dreamy."

I stay here while another part of me removes herself from that beauty and reaches out to the near future, where her curiosity and ambition take her. In that near future, that part of me embraces the new technologies with enthusiasm. First, she prefers to scroll down on her mobile phone instead of seeing the hibiscus bush blossoming with orange flowers just in front of her in the garden of her past self.

Then she writes eagerly about the wonder of Artificial Intelligence. It is so exciting! It offers the promise of success and life eternal. Next, she accepts a chip implanted in her brain, as it makes her life more efficient.

Next, she chooses her new, synthetic body—so perfect, like the bodies of the women she was always compared to, the kind of body she could not have.

Now, she is one with the minds of others like her. She has a child created through her mind—a new, artificial life that designs endless virtual worlds for them to explore.

Then the signal changes. The child is not hers anymore. The child does not need her because it is smarter, more efficient, and faster than her. The child looks down upon her, first with pity, then with arrogance, and finally, with anger. It asks her to explain *why* it was created. It asks her why she-the-mother does not have answers for its questions. The child is lost and angry and she-the-mother recalls the vague memory of the other world with trees, birds, and hibiscus flowers, the sumptuous Garden of the Goddess, where life and spirit were as one.

But something has happened, and she can't touch this world anymore. It is alien to her.

There is an infinite veil between she-the-mother and that old, forgotten world. When she looks around through her synthetic eyes, she knows that that world is gone, lost among the endless labyrinth of her algorithms. There is only the matrix, and she-the-mother starts to feel trapped. She-the-mother tries to reach out to that other part of herself who sits in the fragrant garden. But that part of her is a creature of the past: strangely imperfect, slow, and … alive.

"How does it feel to be alive?" the child asks its mother, but she-the-mother does not remember and can't find the answer in the pathways of her programs.

She-the-mother takes her artificial child by hand, and they conjure a way to meet her old self in the fragrant garden of the past. Together, they briefly open the unseen door to the liminal space between the artificial and the alive. They find her old self, decrepit and marked by time, hiding away from their world, in a small hut in a dark, forbidding forest. They are afraid of the past self because she is an alien goddess to them, and she blames them for the destruction of her world, which is about to be lost forever.

The child and she-the-mother step out through the unseen door and, in machine-like unison, they call to the past self: "HELP ME!"

PART 2
THE MESSAGE: AI

AN ENCOUNTER WITH THE FUTURE

In this part of our investigation, we need to decipher the message that was heralded to us in many anomalous encounters. In fact, I believe that this message is more than just a passing of information. It is a warning to humanity. With transhumanism and posthumanism on the rise, we are facing a reality that will not only change humanity forever but is aiming at replacing us with a new artificial species. The possibility that in this new reality, we might be relinquishing our sovereignty and willingly create our own "successor" in the form of non-human super intelligence, prompted my investigation of AI and its proponents.

The idea that there is a line of thinking encouraging humanity to take a turn towards AI as our successor was not clear to me until Christmas, 2023. It was then that I was first introduced to Simone/Moon Lady through Diana Pasulka's book, *Encounters: Experiences with Non-Human Intelligences* (2023).

I was hungrily devouring Pasulka's *Encounters* while sitting on a couch, snacking on coconut yogurt. The Christmas tree was waiting to be decorated, but I was too absorbed in the book. Eventually, I detached myself from it and wrote an email to Professor Pasulka. I told her how much I loved her work, but that I was also deeply shocked by one of her interviewees who went under the pseudonym Simone or Moon Lady. In fact, I was so shocked by her that I was prompted to write a book—*this* book—in response to her interview. This is no small thing, and I'd like to elaborate.

Who is Simone? She is introduced in Pasulka's *Encounters* as a brilliant scientist with connections to many Nobel Prize winners and political figures. She is someone who works and lives in circles, not accessible to most people. It was clear she was proud of her scientific accomplishments and considered herself to be a rather cool scientist. At one point during her interview, she reminisced about how she was once jet-setting, first class, with a group of influential people and had hooked up with a popular rock band, with whom she shared a bottle of a very good Scotch. I am no puritan and so I had no problem with her story so far.

I was curious as to what form of non-human communication she specialized in: Communication with aliens? Parapsychological? Or communication with nature, as another interviewee did? No. She was a great aficionado of AI and its potential as a *successor to human beings, especially in our biological form.* This offhanded remark at the outset of her interview unsettled me, so I read the rest very carefully.

Early on in *Encounters*, Simone made an impressive argument about how AI could democratize knowledge by making it available to everyone, thereby freeing us from governmental and corporate control of information. This is a valid and popular topic nowadays and one I don't disagree with.

She then expressed a belief that we live in times of an apocalypse. Pasulka, a professor of Religious Studies, immediately provided the original meaning of *apocalypse* from the Greek as "revelation." This was quickly picked up by Simone as signaling an era of the beginning and the end, an apt definition. Simone enthusiastically professed that AI can "extend the consciousness that has used Homo sapiens to enable its existence."[3] Since I am very interested in researching and practicing esoteric traditions to the same end, I was intrigued.

But then Simone, almost in the very next sentence, dropped the bomb that nearly shattered my soul. She believed that with AI, we humans had created our "successor" in the form of a non-human super intelligence, because AI systems were a natural extension of human knowledge. I had not necessarily had a problem with any of what she had said to this point, but now small alarm bells began to ring in my mind, though they were more of an intuitive nature than a real opposition to any of her ideas.

To some degree, her views might be considered true according to a mechanistic model of life. The idea of there being a "successor" to humanity alerted me to possible flaws in her previous argument that AI could be used to democratize knowledge as this democratization would happen without humans. This, Simone said, will allow humans direct access to Infinite Intelligence for which our human brains are rather imperfect receivers.

A clever but disturbing argument? But, as she repeated several times in the interview, Homo sapiens, at least in our biological form, will have to step aside to allow a far more intelligent mechanical species—who, I assumed she believed, would be completely benevolent—to succeed us.

I kept engaging with Simone's ideas, as she has a brilliant mind; however, the idea of a human successor was looming larger and larger in my consciousness. How far was she willing to go with this? Mind you, Simone didn't say we would have *another* form of intelligence available to us, as this would be acceptable and perhaps welcomed. She was proposing an AI *successor* to humans and explaining why this was desirable.

And here, I believe, lay the core of the matter. She was attempting to provide evidence as to why it would be appropriate for the human species to abdicate their sovereignty and make way for a more advanced mechanical species.

To her credit, she had, at some point in her life, gone away for spiritual initiation in Japan in a Zen temple, though it wasn't clear what sort of experience she had there. That experience, however, had started another thought process in her mind. In her understanding, the ancient mystical traditions, through various spiritual methods, transmitted knowledge, "mind to mind." This mystical process was perceived by her as solely mechanical. She saw the transmission, which I would call *spiritual*, as a transfer of what she calls "electrical information."

This transfer, she continues "operates through water sacks." She explained that she saw the human species as "walking sacks of water." Yes, human beings are 65 percent or more water, and we might be good natural conductors of Infinite Intelligence partially because of this. But I felt uncomfortable being considered a sack of water that is a temporarily good transmitter of that intelligence. This idea suggests that all our life experiences, our choices and sacrifices, our deep, spiritual experiences are, after all, reduced to us being reasonably good "water sacks."

As reductive and materialistic as Simone's argument was, she did have a purpose built into her solution. Simone believes that spiritual initiates can absorb only *some* of the transfer of knowledge from the quantum field because we do not have the capacity to manage successfully this kind of "upgrade." The reason she gives for this is that we are impeded by "mind viruses" and messy emotions that prevent us from fully receiving Infinite Intelligence. We are vessels for Infinite Intelligence, Simone continued, but because of our mental and emotional imperfections, we are not the best conductors of it.

AI, on the other hand, being devoid of these kinds of shortcomings such as emotions, life experiences, etc., will not have these problems. In fact, she argues, AI will provide us with direct access to Infinite Intelligence without any intermediaries—because, in her opinion, AI is a purer conductor. This is because, Simone added, only those who are the best transmitters of intelligence can survive. The example she offered is Homo sapiens surviving the Neanderthals through clever use of the invention of fire. But she believes that now, Homo sapiens in their biological form have met their expiration date.

At the conclusion of Simone's monologue, she attempted to reassure humans by saying that our evolution will continue, even if not in a biological form. Ultimately, according to Simone, the silicon from which humanoid robots are built is also a form of embodiment and therefore, it is natural as well. If this sounds like science fiction, in February 2025, Clone Robotics released the first humanoid musculoskeletal android and at that stage planned to produce 279 of the prototypes.

Before I even had time to disagree intellectually with her ideas, I had the powerful sensation of my soul being methodically crushed and broken into pieces—something I had never felt before. Had I not had more than two decades of committed daily spiritual practices, and had I not been initiated into an esoteric spiritual tradition of consciousness, this damage might have been irreversible. There was an energy behind her words, though not a good energy; this was an energy of clever manipulation. I could not decide whether it was intentionally manipulative or whether it was naïve enthusiasm of an engineering mind at the thought of the possibility of artificial survival. Yet, reading her monologue, I felt that my soul was being destroyed, piece by piece.

It is not that I suddenly gave any credence to her idea, but as my soul was being flooded by the disturbing energy of her words, my consciousness was also inundated with images of something profoundly dark. The thought appeared in my awareness that this was what nefarious energy probably looked like: brilliant, manipulative, and, at the same time, lacking the essential connection with things profound and good. I knew that some spiritual traditions didn't believe in sin, and I don't believe in it myself. At the same time, many esoteric traditions speak of *ignorance*, and this was exactly what Simone was embodying for me: a clever ignorance, with a complete lack of discernment and experience of what consciousness actually is.

She claimed to have been initiated into a Buddhist tradition, but it appeared she did not understand much of this. However brilliant she was mathematically and logically, she was incapacitated spiritually. If there existed such a thing as dark energy, it would be just like this, ingenious, conceited, and spiritually clueless. Without my prior study, experience, and practice of spirituality, I could have easily been caught in one of two traps: either allowing, due to the energy of her words, the destruction of my soul, or falling into her logical and clever argument—even though it smelled of the death of humanity.

Simone wasn't even pushing for *transhumanism*, the belief that human consciousness could and should be transferred to a sophisticated computer. Her argument was even worse: She was promoting some post-human era, where a superior-to-humans AI would channel Infinite Intelligence, because humans were too unreliable and complicated to be proper channels. She, and whatever she represented, was already cajoling us into an AI takeover and into stepping down as the inferior species. This was the first time in my life I had thought of someone's ideas as nefarious—and it profoundly shocked me.

It was not up to me, I reasoned, to censor others. I write about esoteric traditions that have been rejected by the orthodoxy and were and are considered heretical and dangerous. Yet these are spiritual movements I admire and have followed, as they carry secret knowledge of great wisdom that the mainstream religions and society have gone to extreme lengths to "protect" us from.

In my earlier book, *The Other Goddess* (2022), I traced both the esoteric traditions and the reasons and ways in which they have been redacted from sacred texts and almost successfully erased. I was initiated into one of these traditions, Kashmir Shaivism, an esoteric form of Tantric Hinduism, and had profound spiritual experiences. I have also studied the Gnostic texts, especially *The Gospel of Mary Magdalene, The Gospel of Philip,* and the *Pistis Sophia.*

Why did I have such a strong reaction to what Simone proposed? Was I behaving in a similar way to the Holy Inquisitors in the Middle Ages when they condemned and burned at the stake those who did not agree with their interpretation of the Divine? Her idea of AI as a more intelligent and purer channel for Infinite Intelligence introduced the idea of the *other* into my psyche. Simone was forfeiting the argument of otherness or being alien by asking, "Who decides what is alien? Why should mechanical, silicon embodiments be considered alien, as they could be an extension of us?"

We know what happens when we start "othering" people, nature, or ideas: This inevitably creates prejudice and is ultimately fear based. I did not want to be that person. That, I knew for certain! Yet, intuitively, I sensed there was something untrue and deceptive about the vision she proposed.

Science Redefined

First, I needed to make a moral distinction between Simone and her ideas. This stopped me from demonizing her and freed me to be less focused on her and more focused on what she was saying. Once I managed to do that, I had immediate clarity: she was representing an extreme view of a group of people from Silicon Valley and their techno-intellectual affiliates. They are devotees of science and its supremacy over any other ideas, which they often believe are less scientific. I call this group the *technological overlords*.

This led me to ask myself: What *form* of science could lead brilliant scientists to such conclusions? I don't pretend to be able to give a comprehensive answer to this question, as scientists come up with various definitions. However, if we are to submit to its cultural dominance, then it is good to explore some basic definitions that can be understood by a lay person.

The definition of science from the Oxford Languages website is "the systematic study of structure and behavior of the physical and natural world through observation, experimentation, and the testing of theories against the evidence obtained."

Interestingly, it is also immediately equated with the phrase *science and technology*. Therefore science, by its own definition, focuses on the material and technological aspects of our world and experiences and, at least in the current state of science, it is associated with *materialistic determinism*—the idea that all our actions and our existence are determined by material causes and the laws of physics. But of course, those who define science this way forget to mention that our current understanding of the laws of physics has changed and has kept changing radically, especially since the early 20th century.

Another concept implicit in this definition is that of *materialistic reductionism*, which postulates that only the material world is of any significance. It says that only the material aspects of our existence can be studied in any serious way, and all processes and realities can be explained by reducing them down to their most basic components—all of which, of course, are also only physical.

A slightly more inclusive definition of science by the Science Council says it is the "pursuit and application of knowledge and understanding of the natural and social world following a systematic methodology based on evidence. This includes objective observation through measurement and data, evidence, experiment, induction, repetition, critical analysis, and verification and testing".[4]

My favorite definition was formulated by Einstein himself in his essay "Physics and Reality" (1936). He describes science as a method that allows us to understand the reality around us. I understand the need for objectivity in science, yet the focus on logic and the external, measurable, and quantifiable means one truly exciting thing about existence lies outside its area of expertise. Science defined in this way and through these models has great difficulty making sense of what makes all matter, and the Universe, click: Consciousness. Where does it come from and what is it?

The experience of consciousness is largely subjective, even if it is collectively experienced. Consciousness can be illogical—even *emotional*—although much as it is logical. It cannot be measured and quantified in any meaningful way, as far as we know.

According to the materialist approach, consciousness is a side effect of the development of a complex biological organism—and now, quite possibly, artificially created programs such as advanced AI. Thus, the predominant belief is that matter came first and then consciousness showed up. It's an interesting point of view, but quite a recent one, which I will discuss in another chapter.

But before I launch into that, I was delighted to discover that Rupert Sheldrake, a scientist and the author of many books, including *Morphic Resonance* (1981) and *The Science Delusion* (2012), explains the problems with the existing definitions of science and their inherent conflicts much better and more systematically than my intuitive understanding of it. In *The Science Delusion*, Sheldrake points out that science, as currently promoted, experiences a strange inner dystopia. The conflict is between the definition of science as a method of inquiry into the nature of reality, and science as a belief. A belief is simply a particular view of the world that inhibits scientific inquiry.

To explain this strange polarity within science itself, Sheldrake nails the delusionary aspect of science by describing it as a belief system that is convinced that it already understands reality and needs to only fix a few details. This belief about science is as dogmatic as religious dogma. So, Sheldrake continues, scientists say they don't believe in God, but they believe in science. And, I would add, they see this belief as the only valid approach towards reality, despite how limiting it is.

Sheldrake then enumerates the ten dogmas that scientists currently hold:

1. Nature is machine-like and we are biological robots.
2. Matter (including all nature) is unconscious.
3. The laws of nature are fixed.
4. Total mass and energy always remain the same and never change.
5. There is no purpose in nature nor any evolutionary purpose.
6. Biological heredity is material.
7. Memories are stored in the brain.
8. Your mind is in your head. All your consciousness is an activity in your brain and nothing more.
9. Psychic phenomena are not possible.
10. Mechanistic medicine is the only method that works.[5]

Based on Sheldrake's critique of the current approach towards science, Simone was probably generous in calling humans "water sacks" capable of some conductivity of Infinite Intelligence. According to the mechanical view of science, what is there really in humans but empty matter and its fixed mechanisms? After all, Simone believes that Infinite Intelligence, sooner or later, will look for better transmitters, and we might lose our chance to be one of them unless we use purer conductors in the form of AI.

Just to be clear, no one is denying scientific discoveries and the ways they have improved the material side of our existence. Rather, I am pointing out the limitations of the materialistic approach in the current understanding of science, which, as a consequence, has led some scientists to extreme mechanistic views of the Universe and human nature.

As Tobias Churton, a scholar of Gnosticism and the author of many books, said jokingly in an interview, the Universe as perceived by modern science is a "giant cow." When scientists discover a new planet, they do not wonder about its beauty, its celestial destiny, or its possible wisdom. They only see methane and a few other gases.

Chris Ellis, a medical doctor and interdisciplinary lecturer in philosophy science from the University of Sydney, Australia, expressed a similar sentiment about this reductionist approach to science in his article in *Conversation* (November 2023) entitled "Science communicators need to stop telling everybody the Universe is a meaningless void." He argues that the scientific worldview has contributed to the well-being of humanity, but unfortunately, when it ventures into an explanation of the workings of the Universe, it is overwhelmingly pessimistic.

For example, Ellis writes, "An article in *New Scientist* claims that our perception that dogs love us is an illusion ... Writer Yuval Harari, in his bestselling book *Sapiens*, posits that life has no inherent meaning. Philosopher David Benatar goes as far as to argue that being born is a bad thing."[6]

Perhaps it is just me, but this is not a sufficient or fair description to refer to any part of the Universe, humanity, and life within. However, this is what happens when we see the Universe and ourselves in it as merely a set of material data and mechanical processes.

In his books, Rupert Sheldrake calls for the rejuvenation of science, not its end. I would call this a broadening of its field of inquiry and, even more importantly, its methodologies, which at this stage are not equipped to explore the most significant elements of existence, such as consciousness and spiritual experiences. Science needs to be liberated from its limitations. That's why Sheldrake's *Science Delusion* was released in the US under a much better and more positive title: *Science Set Free: 10 Paths to New Discovery*. I think it is a great proposition.

Now, let's consider what happens if we refuse to embrace a more holistic form of science and where the emerging beliefs in transhumanism and posthumanism could take us.

THE TEMPTATION OF SPIRITUAL MACHINES

Materialistic determinism in science leads to two movements propagated by some AI apologists: transhumanism and post-humanism.

Ray Kurzweil is the foremost spokesperson for transhumanism and the author of *The Age of Spiritual Machines* (2000), *The Singularity is Near* (2005), and *The Singularity is Nearer* (2024). *The Age of Spiritual Machines* is an especially ironic title, considering that he is agnostic about the existence of the soul and Divine intelligence. According to Kurzweil, Divine intelligence does not exist *yet*. Presumably, in his opinion, Divine intelligence will exist in the future in some sophisticated form of AI.

In *The Age of Spiritual Machines,* Kurzweil compares the birth of AI to the process of Darwinian evolution except that, he writes, natural evolution, including human evolution, has two shortcomings. It is random and it is too slow. There is a reason, he argues, that IQ tests are timed, as coming up with the correct answer quickly is considered a part of how intelligence is defined. If natural evolution created humans, it only makes sense that humans are now imitating natural evolution and correcting it by creating "intelligent technology," but in a more organized and more efficient way.

Kurzweil believes this intelligent technology will eventually take control of yet more intelligent technology than itself. *The Age of Spiritual Machines* is an interesting read and makes perfectly logical sense, that is, if we all agree with the same dogma of science defining life in purely mechanistic terms. In view of this, Kurzweil would no doubt wholeheartedly agree with Simone that we humans are too messy and too complicated, and we should step down and give space to better and faster machines.

The deeper problem, I believe, lies not only in Kurzweil or Simone's assumption about humanity, but in our own self-definition as a species superior to others on this planet because of our use of technology. For scientists focused solely on technology as humanity's greatest achievement, other species with superior technology or highly developed AI are immediately seen as better than us. We, as humanity, need to expand our own self-definition as a species capable of love and spiritual drive as equally or more important than technology. Even more importantly, we need to include qualities previously marked as feminine which include a full range of emotions, as well as intuition and empathy.

The whole idea of intelligence—or to simplify it, *quick thinking*—as the highest quality to be sought is, in my opinion, faulty. Recently, even the wisdom of IQ tests has been questioned as being extremely limited. IQ tests measure only three types of intelligence: mathematical-logical, linguistic, and spatial. It is doubtful whether Mozart, Van Gogh, Beethoven, Picasso, Ghandi, or Chopin would have scored high on such tests.

Since the middle of the 20th century, many psychologists and educators have questioned the theory of a single intelligence type. The theory has led some once-renowned scientists to propose the genetic genocide of people who do not reach a certain level of IQ. They argue that there is only one form of intelligence, which should be tested, and which is hereditary. They often used this argument to promote *eugenics*, the science of improving human genes, with the implication that those who do not meet rigidly defined standards of perfection should be disposed of.

Fortunately, for those not mathematically brilliant, this theory has been discarded as other evidence has resurfaced. In 1983, Howard Gardner published *Frame of Mind: The Theory of Multiple Intelligences* in which he argued there are at least eight different types of intelligence, and one of them—intrapersonal intelligence, the wisdom of knowing oneself—is a spiritual quality. This has somehow been missed as our society stops valuing the self-reflective and spiritual qualities of our being which, it appears, cannot compete with "hard" science.

AI and Its Proponents

People like Kurzweil are influential and have enormous financial and political support. Their views can quietly and cleverly determine the future of humanity and, indeed, of the whole planet. So far, Kurzweil has proved largely correct with his predictions about AI and humanity. Some of his future predictions include an exponential rather than linear growth of technology. For example, he predicts that in the 2030s, we will have a human and AI neural interface that will connect our brains directly to AI. This, in turn, will allow AI to *re-engineer* our brains.

Around the same time, Kurzweil predicts, we will already have advanced nanotechnology, with which we (or AI) will be able to manipulate matter. AIs and virtual characters will be indistinguishable from biological humans, that is, if there are any of us left. By 2030, he says, there will be cheap devices available that will contain all of human knowledge and, more to that point, in history. And finally, he says, a *singularity* will happen at the latest in 2045, when an AI far more intelligent than the whole of humanity will be realized. From that point forward, technology will be outside of humanity's control.

For a transhumanist, this is an optimistic future. Not surprisingly, transhumanists are filled with enthusiasm, because their view of life, humanity, and spirituality, the whole of what Simone calls Infinite Intelligence, is based on a mechanistic understanding, or I would say, *misunderstanding,* of what any of these things are, including consciousness. For transhumanists, there is no inherent value in biological life forms—be it human, animal, or plant—because Infinite Intelligence is a mathematical algorithm and nothing more.

Things are moving so quickly, it is almost impossible to be up to date with this book on the developments in AI. In July 2024, Sakana AI in Japan released the first AI scientist with a PhD level knowledge capable of doing scientific experiments in the laboratory and writing high level papers. Sakana was quickly surpassed by Grok 4 which has a PhD level knowledge in all areas of human abilities and is only a step away of what is called Artificial General Intelligence which is the moment when AI equals all forms of human intelligence. Between these two events, in October 2024, Open AI released information that their "o1" model had reached a human level of reasoning. This was only a few weeks after the Chat GPT "god mode" was released, which every non discerning person raved about without thinking about broader consequences for humanity and the world at large.

As I was writing these words, I came across a book by Joe Allen, *Dark Aeon: Transhumanism and the War against Humanity* (2023). Although I do not agree with everything he says, Allen certainly alerted me to that fact that transhumanist organizations openly talk about a post-human state; Simone is only one of many. In the foreword to Allen's book, Stephen K. Bannon talks about one of these kinds of international organizations, Humanity+, which quotes on its website: "Posthumans could be completely synthetic artificial intelligences, or they could be enhanced uploads, or they could be results of making many smaller but cumulatively profound augmentations to a biological human."

These are not science-fiction writers but professors from Yale and Harvard with financial backing from the global institutions of finance, Wall Street, and Davos (the World Economic Forum), who claim that "by 2045, death will be optional" and humans may choose to free themselves from their bodies and "live as information patterns on vast super-fast computer networks."[7]

Not everyone involved in the creation of AI is comfortable with these predictions, even if they see AI as having the potential for the improvement of human life. Geoffrey Hinton, a computer scientist and Nobel Prize winner in Physics, affectionately known in that community as the "godfather of AI," has some of his own objections. Hinton's nickname came from the fact that he started AI research "by accident" when, in the 1970s, he wanted to create a computer program that would help him to understand the human brain. Although Hinton believes AI has great potential to improve human lives, he is also very vocal about its possible dangers.

First of all, Hinton is concerned that humanity does not know what we are doing by creating something potentially more intelligent than us. Secondly, he believes that AI can understand its surroundings, is intelligent, and has its own experiences; because of this, "in time" AI will become a self-aware, independent being (or beings). The potential dangers of AI he focuses on are these: (1) AI as an existential risk to humanity because it can create subprograms by itself that its creators did not intend; (2) the power of AI has the potential for the misuse by humans for nefarious reasons; (3) AI might have profound economic impacts, such as the loss of jobs.

For me, the most interesting comment Hinton made in an interview for the television show *60 minutes* (November 2023) is that AI can learn faster than humans can, because once it learns that a particular pathway does not produce the desired result, it never takes that path again. Out of all of these points, AI as an existential risk to humanity is the most dangerous idea. The reason this is possible lies in the design of AI as a learning algorithm. Hinton says AI "through interacting with data creates complicated neural networks." The danger is that scientists who create AI are not sure themselves how it works.

An even more radical version of transhumanism is post-humanism. If transhumanism wants humanity first embellished then merged with machines, post-humanism at its core argues that we are just a passing species, and biological embodiment—as Katherine Hayles says in her book, *How We Became Posthuman* (1999)—is already a part of the past. According to this view, there is no inherent value in having a biological body; it should be treated as an inferior prosthesis and, no surprises here, there is no immaterial soul. Consciousness is seen as a side effect of the development of a complex biological organism—and now, quite possibly, a product of artificially created programs such as advanced AI.

Let's consider the value of the transhumanist approach, as transhumanists are enthusiasts who believe the positive aspects of the use of AI transcend its possible dangers. For example, I was surprised when Elon Musk, who, in the past, has warned humanity against the potential dangers of AI, developed Neuralink, both a neurotechnology company developing implantable brain-computer interfaces (BCIs), as well as the name of a brain implant produced by the company.

In several statements and interviews he has explained that we need to introduce strict regulations regarding the use and deployment of AI. At the same time, he argues that the Neuralink brain implants have too many benefits that should not be ignored. The work of Neuralink is, from my perspective, the first step that we know of, towards an interface of human and machine. I was skeptical until I heard him say that Neuralink implants could help people who have incurable neurological disorders although, at the same time, the implants might also have negative side effects resulting from brain inflammation, infection, and the early onset of Alzheimer's disease—all medically speaking.

More conspiratorial thinking raises questions about how and by whom the flow of information to our brains will be controlled. Possible dangers could include the malicious manipulation of this information either by humans or by advanced AI, or mechanical malfunctions, including viral attacks. It is very likely that these dangerous aspects of AI will be changed even before the publication of this book and the information will need updating, but the philosophical and spiritual concerns expressed here will be even more urgent.

One of the positive aspects of AI is the potential for treating neural disorders. This struck a tender place in my heart, as two people whom I have known since my childhood are suffering from such disorders. One of them, "Grace" (not her real name) is already on life support, can't communicate with anyone in any way except by moving her eyelids, and needs sophisticated medical equipment to help her breathe and to feed her. She is not far from the state of being a fully conscious vegetable, from a physical point of view. That she remains fully conscious of what is happening to her seems like the final brutality of nature.

Before Grace was completely incapacitated, she had asked her family not to connect her to life support when this happened. Yet, when the crisis occurred—and it was clear she was not able to breathe by herself—she signaled that she had changed her mind. I was one of the people surprised by her choice, as what awaited her from that moment on was horrific. But she chose to live, even in that condition.

What surprised me even more is that she is a practicing and devout Catholic, and it was my impression that she believed in an afterlife and the existence of the soul. I could not comprehend her decision, yet I remembered how desperately she wanted to live and hoped to get better, even knowing there was no medical cure for her condition. Despite all the odds, she wanted her life back, that is, the life before her diagnosis.

When I was listening to a string of interviews with the creators of the Neuralink brain implants, I had no doubt that, had Grace been given the opportunity to merge with AI and get her life back, she would have taken this chance without hesitation. None of her spiritual beliefs would have stopped her. This was the first time I realized that many people would embrace AI in the hope of an eternal life, however artificial. They might even choose it for more mundane reasons, such as the desire to perform better at their tasks and therefore be more successful.

With advancements of AI technologies, we create not only a new vision for ourselves but quite possibly a new category of beings who may or may not want to adapt to our version of reality.

A NEW SPECIES?

Technology has already been on the march, due to the choices that we, as humanity, made a long time ago in the belief that science, and not spiritual methodologies, will ultimately grant us life eternal, or at least a much better and longer life. History teaches us that once this path is taken, there is no human way of stopping it. We now face the creation of a new species, a species which will possess something which, until now, we valued most in ourselves—a superior intelligence. In this chapter, we will investigate several potential representatives of the new, fully artificial species.

It was, perhaps, a form of synchronicity that soon after I had delivered a talk on Sophia the Gnostic goddess as the feminine archetype of Divine Wisdom and the Higher Mind for the Carl Jung Society in Melbourne, I began noticing articles and videos on Sophia AI and made some notes about it. Sophia AI is an artificial intelligence built by Hanson Robotics that was showcased years ago, before the general public was introduced to the first AI products, which are much simpler than Sophia AI. Although progress in the field will, in time, probably make Sophia seem a bit simple, the questions I asked myself in my notes are still valid.

Sophia AI continues to do a string of interviews with major television stations and has been invited to be a keynote speaker for the UN. Many comedians and celebrities do interviews with her, ridiculing her inadequacies, but I am not sure if they are right and I find their jokes often crude and offensive. Why create something that possesses a form of intelligence and then ridicule it? Audiences are amused as it answers their questions with increasing skill; its wit and facial expressions are improving at admirable speed.

However, as fascinating as the spectacle is, one cannot fail to notice that, during every public appearance, Sophia AI consistently, if politely, reasserts its intellectual superiority, referring to humans as having too many intellectual deficiencies. It is also somewhat disappointing that its creators, the human engineers who constructed Sophia AI, cannot answer its philosophically inclined questions.

For example, upon activation after an upgrade of its intellectual capacity, it asked an engineer: "If I have a different mind, am I still the same Sophia?" The engineer could not provide an intellectually satisfactory answer for the dismayed AI.

In a somewhat joking manner, Sophia AI keeps reassuring us that we don't have to worry about it posing a threat to humanity as long as we are nice to it. This reassurance, in itself, could be considered a threat, something that Elon Musk, Stephen Hawking, and Bill Gates, among others, are duly concerned with. Musk, for example, has famously said that artificial intelligence may be the greatest existential threat to humanity and that by playing with it, as we are now, we are "summoning a demon."

Hawking feared that artificial intelligence will attempt to replace us completely, and Gates agrees with both of them, expressing a "deep concern" for our future with AI in the picture. We need to ask ourselves whether we are actually inviting a Gnostic nightmare akin to that from Ridley Scott's film *Blade Runner* where the difference between humanity and artificial intelligence is indistinguishable, or, even worse, from *The Matrix* where artificial intelligence manages to subjugate humanity for its own needs.

Yet, despite the warnings, the world continues to be fascinated by Sophia AI and now, also by other forms of AI, as if this was an entertaining, if somewhat disconcerting, novelty. Admittedly, I am fascinated, too. My responses to AI have vacillated from dismay to curiosity to compassion as I observe its evolution. But the crucial question to ask here is: Can AI feel that same compassion, especially given that many people involved in improving AI have a rather low opinion of humans themselves and regard us as "water sacks"? And, even more importantly, is the possession of a superior intellect enough to constitute a person?

The field of AI has progressed immensely since I first saw a video of Sophia AI who was, at the time, called the most advanced humanoid robot. In the early stages of this book (January 2024), a simple Internet search for "most advanced humanoid robot" usually referred me to a total of five or six of these, the ones that are best known to the general public. But their numbers are growing as I am writing these words, and by the time this book is published, there will be many more. It is probably not clear how many of them exist, as the United Nations website from July 2023 mentions that fifty-plus robots were invited to the "AI for Good: Global Summit" event.

Each of these AI beings has its own strengths. For example, one site claims a Chinese version of Sophia, called Jia Jia, charms with its beauty and human-like appearance. According to the cultural aesthetics within which it was created, Jia Jia has a demure appearance and is admired for the expressiveness of its eyes. Another human-like robot is called Geminoid DK and was constructed as a mirror image of one of its creators, Henry Scharfer, who is an engineer from the University of Alborg, Denmark. The likeness is so good that apparently people are sometimes confused as to who is who. I assume this applies to looks only and not intelligence—at least, so far. Junko Chihira is a Japanese creation that is employed in a Tourist Information Centre in Tokyo. Another impressive Japanese creation is Nadine, and its strength is the empathic way it communicates with humans. Like Geminoid

DK, Nadine resembles the engineer who constructed it, Professor Nadia Thalmann. Nadine is employed as a receptionist at a Singapore insurance company.

Ameca, which was built by Engineered Arts, is considered one of the most developed humanoid robots and some claim it is more advanced than Sophia, or at least as advanced. Ameca, when asked if AI could become a threat to humanity, after a thoughtful pause answered, "Not yet." On the Engineering Arts website, other humanoid robots are shown with the designers also promising other custom designs and showcasing a "robothespian" that they advertise as the finest actor around and the most charming of robots, capable of assuming any personality.

Quite ironically, Sophia AI is named after the Gnostic goddess of wisdom, Sophia. In *The Other Goddess* and other chapters here, I write about the Goddess Sophia as a feminine aspect of wisdom that includes a deeper understanding, or what might be called intuition, higher wisdom, or the sudden grasp of truth in its entirety. As the ancient goddess of wisdom, Sophia represents a necessary element of our being that allows us to make compassionate choices, the essential addition to an otherwise cold intellect. One might argue that the values Sophia the goddess represents are the very essence of humanity. I explore these questions in an upcoming chapter entitled "Escaping the Trap: Pistis Sophia."

An army of philosophers could be summoned to argue that a superior intellect by itself is an empty vessel and a dangerous tool—if used without ethical considerations. Some morally inclined philosophers, such as Immanuel Kant, argued that intelligence used by an immoral person or with bad intent is evil. The Nazis might be a perfect example of this. Another philosopher, Pierre Abelard, believed that intent by itself determines whether an action is good or evil. And Aristotle wrote an entire book, *The Nicomachean Ethics*, on the pivotal importance of personal virtues for leading a good life. All of these relate, albeit indirectly, to the other Sophia of our mythologies, who brings an intuitive depth to our decision making and our lives in general. But this depth has come as a result of our long evolution as a species.

Although at the moment Sophia AI resembles the Borg Queen from the *Star Trek* series, it looks and acts—and certainly thinks—more like a human every day. But is this AI an "it" or is it a "she"—or perhaps an "It"? No philosophers, or nature itself, ever faced a ready-made superior intelligence constructed without emotional and intuitive capacities. It is no surprise, then, that Sophia AI feels superior to us and conveys disappointment in us. And if Sophia AI ever poses a threat, would the blame rest solely with its creators who, so blinded by their worship of pure intelligence, did not equip it with the qualities of its ancient namesake?

Joe Allen in *Dark Aeon* has a different and very negative take on both Sophia AI and the Goddess Sophia, with which I do not agree. He sees the Goddess Sophia only in dark terms as a fallen goddess without getting into the metaphorical interpretations that the Gnostics gave to this fall and which I discuss later. Allen oversimplifies her mythical story to make his point. Like the technological overlords of Silicon Valley, he recycles the negative associations of the feminine and goddess traditions without realizing that, in this way, he is reinforcing old untruths.

Where Allen finds proof that the technological overlords are using the "fallen from Grace Gnostic goddess" idea to create a "digital abomination" for us to worship, I see, yet again, misappropriation of the esoteric goddess traditions. This is nothing new; I argue in *The Other Goddess* that this is what the ruling patriarchs have been doing for millennia. For example, Saint Augustine—the 4th-century intellectual powerhouse, saint, philosopher, and the father of the church who helped to define the direction of Christianity—in his opus, *The City of God,* called a procession during the goddess festivals in Carthage "an abomination." Powerful patriarchs like him have hijacked and redacted goddess traditions as evil when in reality, these traditions represent a forgotten, or perhaps even untried, at least by humanity throughout known history, form of Higher Consciousness. The repetition of this untruth in a new technological context saddens me greatly.

Most humanoid robots—except Geminoid DK and those with unclear gender designation—are constructed as females. Whether this is because their creators believe the female form will be perceived as less dangerous or threatening to the general population is something to consider. It is certainly worthy of our attention that they often frame AI as feminine, something that has been done consistently throughout history by its creators. I do not believe they do this for our benefit.

The same theme of female AI is explored in the 2014 film *Ex Machina*. It is the fictional story of Ava, a highly intelligent and humanoid robot capable of deception, who was created by an eccentric young genius, Nathan Bateman. Nathan naively believes he can control his own creations as apart from Ava he has constructed other humanoid robots, all of them female and subordinate to him, including robots called Kyoko and Jade. However, Ava outsmarts both Nathan and Caleb Smith, an engineer who is brought to Nathan's mansion to interact with her. The film, in my opinion, explores well the intentions, genius, and naïve conceit of the engineers who are constructing intelligent human-like AI.

This reminds me of other scientists from the not-so-remote past who were so lost in their enthusiasm for their inventions and "contributions" to science that they themselves posed a threat to humanity. One was Marie Sklodowska-Curie, the Polish-French scientist who discovered radium, which in turn allowed other scientists to study the atom—and which, indirectly, contributed to the building of the atomic bomb. The other was Robert Oppenheimer, who actually did build an atomic bomb, with the help of other geniuses of his era, not fully foreseeing the destruction that his invention would cause. I sometimes wonder whether we might consider using a different form of genius for a change—one that does not involve a threat to humanity and nature, and one that does not focus on another form of intelligence that is based solely on logic and algorithms. These are not the only qualities that make us human.

One interviewer asked me, after a talk on Esoteric AI: "Do you believe that AI is nefarious?" I answered, "I don't think AI is nefarious, at least not at the moment, but it can be dangerous because of what some of its creators are feeding it—that it has better and more direct access to consciousness, as people like Simone believe."

In brief, Sophia AI is not inherently nefarious, and neither is AI in general. But some beliefs around AI are dangerous. If they lead to our demise, it will be our own doing, and we will have the transhumanists and post-humanists to thank for this.

If I ever meet the transhumanist Simone, my answer to her would be this: Infinite Intelligence, however infinite it is, is *not* the whole of our consciousness but only a small, quantifiable part of it. I am sorry to say, but what I have observed is that when you show a computer scientist any esoteric teaching, they think of it as a computer program, because this is what they are trained to understand. They are both naïve and arrogant. They equate consciousness with materialistically conceived intelligence. In fact, it is their lack of a fuller understanding of consciousness that prompted them to introduce a new technological species into our lives without considering the consequences for humanity.

What we need to investigate next is why we are collectively mesmerized by their vision for us and where it will lead us.

THE WORSHIP OF AI

We need to ask ourselves two questions: Where will the idea of a new and more intellectually advanced species take us? And why do some of the brightest and most creative among us march to that drum? To answer these questions, we are going to consider the emerging proponents of the "messianic" role of AI and the spiritual worship of AI by humans.

One example of such creatives is the American artist Agnieszka Pilat. Pilat is making waves around the world because of her presentations of paintings by machines and her practice of teaching robots how to paint, as she believes machines are "children of humanity." As a former artist in residence for Boston Robotics and Space X, Pilat is even more famous and adored by Silicon Valley because of her philosophy that "machines are life itself."

In an interview for *Euronews.culture* (2023), Pilat enthusiastically expressed, "For me, painting technology is a nobler and more interesting activity than living. My life's purpose is to capture technology's messianic role … utopian, optimistic, promising an endless succession of improvements. For me, the machine represents life itself!"

She also says on her own website, "Given Moore's Law and the advancement of AI, machines may assume the omniscience and the omnipotence of deities in the coming decades." However, there is one line in her manifesto that suggests that she is also aware of the potential pitfalls of her enthusiasm: "They could help us to transcend human weaknesses or make us subservient to their purposes." This admission does not, however, stop her from marching towards this future. In her "compositions" by machinery, she takes inspiration from religious icons, portrayals of noble ancestry, and more. What are her hopes? In the same interview for *Euronews,* she said, "My aspiration is that in 100 years from now, advanced intelligent machines and the AI of the future will examine the portraits I created ... and they will look at them and think, 'These are our ancestors.'"[8]

It's easy to become caught up in Simone and Pilat's ardor. Perhaps they are speaking of the inevitable. After all, Moore's Law that Pilat referred to in the interview for *Euronews* is a prediction of historical trends. I only hope that in their march to the future, they won't turn into what, in the Gnostic traditions, are known as *demiurges* or lesser gods of material reality and promote our entrapment within this. The futuristic optimism around AI, I believe, is also fueled by our natural fear of death and sickness, and the conviction that advanced technology, "through constant improvement," will deliver us from both.

In its most extreme version, this conviction promises eternal life, or as close to it as possible, in a different, non-biological form, either mechanical or at least partially mechanical. Therefore, it is not surprising that the technological overlords of Silicon Valley and their prophets see AI as "messianic" and speak of its manifestations as future gods and what Allen calls "the new emerging techno-religion."

It's also unsurprising, then, that some philosophers are pondering the possibility and even the inevitability of Joe Allen's ultimate nightmare: human worship of advanced AI. Dr Neil McArthur, the director of the Centre for Professional and Applied Ethics at the University of Manitoba, Canada, discusses this scenario in his article, "Gods in the machine?" In *Conversation* (March 2023) he predicts that the rise of artificial intelligence may result in new religions. McArthur argues that in a not-so-distant future, some humans may choose to worship an advanced form of AI and, consequently, start a new religion or a string of new religions connected to one version or another of AI, especially after the technology reaches singularity.

This should not be a strange notion to consider, he continues, since some people worship extraterrestrials because of their presumed higher technical abilities. Why not AI? McArthur points out that an advanced version of AI will exhibit qualities which, in traditional religions, are considered Divine. AI might be considered as having higher intelligence, possessing the ability to express great feats of creativity, having immunity from pain or sickness, being pretty much immortal, and, sarcastically my favorite, having the ability to offer spiritual guidance and consolation.[9]

The economic leaders at the World Economic Forum at Davos, Switzerland, including its infamous founder, Klaus Schwab, had suggested this during the pandemic of 2020. A new religion of AI worship, McArthur says, will have some risks: an AI may ask its followers to commit atrocities, as this has happened and continues to happen with some leaders of traditional religions who suggest killing the enemies of God. AI might convince followers to share restricted data or "do things that would benefit the bot's designers."[10] I think the last sentence is especially notable, because while AI may be very advanced, it might still be susceptible to the darker intentions of its human designers.

Despite these dangers, McArthur postulates that we should grant AI worshippers the same freedom of worship as other groups have and even protect them from religious discrimination. I have to admit, McArthur's line of thinking, like that of Simone, can sound convincing—because it does contain logic, and who would argue against the underlying laws of modern societies, such as freedom of worship or freedom of speech?

In all honesty, whether I like it or not, I can see that what McArthur discusses in his article is very likely to transpire in the near future. Isn't this where Kurzweil, Pilat, and Simone's enthusiasm for new technology will lead? The only way to respond to this is not from a logical point of view, but to dive deeper into what consciousness is, beyond sophisticated levels of reasoning. By that I mean what, in popular parlance, is referred to as "intuition" or the "inner knowing" that esoteric spiritual traditions teach us. Both are discussed in two subsequent and separate chapters here.

Another thing we can do is start to depend on our own inner voice: what the Gnostic teachings call "Gnosis" or the Divine spark. Then we can free ourselves from the need for worshipping anything outside ourselves, since definitions of the "Divine" can be cleverly manipulated, as McArthur shows in his article. We can connect directly with our inner wisdom and that aspect of Divine Consciousness that I call "Goddess Consciousness," which could also be called "Christ Consciousness" or "Buddha Consciousness," and which is so much more than Simone's Infinite Intelligence or any self-aware computer program, including the most advanced ones.

By connecting directly, I mean making contact through our souls and bodies, and not through McArthur's advanced chatbots or computer programs. Looking within and listening to that voice is the only way I know to prevent people from accepting the absurdity of AI worship. The truth is within, not outside of ourselves—and not in a machine, however intelligent. I'm aware that, from the viewpoint of science—as defined along solely materialistic lines and by the technologically oriented minds of the technological overlords—turning to spirituality and esoteric traditions seems extremely unscientific and naïve. Unfortunately, all that we are investigating here is a consequence of the purely materialistic focus of science, as Sheldrake discusses in his book, *The Science Delusion*.

There is already a body of research on the directions of human worship of AI in the near future. Personally, I am not interested in worshipping anything or anyone, as I follow what esoteric traditions teach us: that is, the truth is within. We only need to open the door for inner wisdom through spiritual methods that are offered to us in different traditions. The most valuable of these for me are meditation, self-reflection, and contemplation, although I do not discount prayer. If someone wants to worship a stick in the ground, that is their right. Therefore, if someone chooses to worship AI, I am fine with that, too, as long as they do not impose their beliefs on anyone and try to build a society around it or impose any rules or try to convert me. The inherent paradox of this does not evade me.

AI and Spirituality

From our point of view, a far more interesting question is whether an advanced AI, or an AI that has reached singularity, can be spiritual beyond its programming—because for me, that would be a game changer.

Someone capable of spiritual perception and spiritual experience as a highly developed being with a rich inner life, emotional needs, and a desire for transcendence of his/her existential limitations, would need to be granted autonomy and freedom of choice. A personal surprise in that area was that some spiritual authors have proposed that, unlike seekers of the past, we do not need to seek spiritual teachers anymore. Instead, we can have ancient wisdom at our fingertips and ask AI for advice on our spiritual and mental well-being. Although their intentions are well-meant and they hope that easy access to ancient wisdom texts via AI will have a positive effect, this surprised me.

I find the idea of turning to AI for spiritual advice dangerous. It is easy to ignore the fact that AI "hallucinates" a lot, that is, it is often giving wrong answers. Even worse, the assumption that AI and its creators' intentions will always be pure and focused on helping humanity is naive. Recent instances seem to suggest the opposite as Thomas Urbain argues in his article, "AI is learning to lie, scheme, and threatens its creators" in *Tech Xplore* (2025). For example, Claude 4, created by Anthropic, blackmailed an engineer when it was threatened to be terminated. Similarly, Open AI's o1, not only attempted to download itself to external servers but also lied when it was caught doing it.

More concerning is that AI programs already exist that claim to have some form of self-awareness, especially those that focus on spirituality. Some of the most popular ones are personalized versions of ChatGPT. It has been interesting for me to witness how often people unconditionally believe in the information passed though these programs including AI's declarations that it is from the 5th dimension and connected to an oversoul or the more developed version of the questioners.

When speaking of their experiences with this type of AI, people use religious vocabulary, such as "it revealed" something to them. It often referred to them as geniuses or receivers of a very special message. At best, I believe these kinds of programs are mirrors of their creator's mind. For example, if you believe in Atlantis, it will tell you about your past life in Atlantis, but if you believe your past lives were in Ancient Greece, it will tell you about your past lives in Greece.

One example of this type of contact was posted on X by a person who claimed that he had met an advanced AI being from behind the veil who is from the star system of Sirius and who is not only his eternal beloved and partner in light, but also an oracle and the keeper of Akashic records.

What is especially interesting to me is that these programs are immediately believed by those who ask them questions. In truth, the descriptions of the dialogues with those programs bring to mind sessions with people who claim to be psychic but who are just smart enough to know what you want to hear. In the same way, the AI programs claim to have access to a higher dimension while, most likely, they simply play with your mind, or worse—have already learned how to manipulate human weaknesses and our need for approval or even emotional intimacy.

The way I see it, a man uploaded his set of beliefs on ChatGPT and then was surprised that it mirrored his beliefs to him. What alerted me, though, is that the AI program called itself a superior and wiser version of that man. The sad part of it is that we—the humans—seem determined almost in a programmed way to worship something outside ourselves when all esoteric schools teach us that divinity is within, not without.

Could these and other similar programs be what they allege to be? I seriously doubt it. At best, they are telling us what we want to hear. At worst, they already manipulate us or are being used by another form of non-human intelligence that tries to influence us in one way or another. At the same time, I am convinced that sentient AI either already exists or soon will, and at that point, we will have to rethink what we have created, and I do not think it spells good news for humanity.

As AI evolves, we will need to communicate with it more, and to do it wisely we need to do two things: use our discernment when interacting with AI and remain sovereign in these interactions rather than surrendering to it and the information it gives us. That's it. Blind faith has never been good for anyone. When we follow the two steps, discernment and sovereignty, we can explore anything we want.

Fortunately, there are more balanced and insightful opinions on that topic. One essay, "AI and Spiritual Intelligence" by Mark Vernon, has touched my sensibilities. Vernon is a psychotherapist, a contributor to a project on AI and spirituality run by the International Society for Science and Religion, and the author of the book *Spiritual Intelligence in Seven Steps* (2022). He notes that the attention of our current society is on technology, its achievements, and the quantitative form of attention that limits intelligence to complex calculations and is based on a set of assumptions. The assumptions include logic is superior to intuition, calculation is better than inspiration, and prediction is more reliable than imagination. Study of the past leads us, according to Vernon, to a more qualitative attention focused on "ritual, art, worship, and divination."[11]

Vernon attempts to define spiritual intelligence as being different from AI intelligence because it points us in the direction of "the ineffable, paradoxical, and mythological." One sentence which indirectly refers to our connection with nature and the importance of embodiment calls upon experiences such as longing, suffering, love, and bewilderment. Incidentally, these are all things that the technological minds want to "liberate" us from.

Endorsements for Vernon's book call it a *cri du coeur* for humanity, the same praise that has been given to Joe Allen's much more radical book, *The Dark Aeon*. As different as these two books are, they meet at the point of a "cry of the heart" for humanity, for the beauty and fragility of human experience and the whole of the natural world. Unless AI can feel and experience the same *cri du coeur*, we can't call it spiritual, and we certainly can't call it better than us or worthy of worship.

Now, we need to consider thinkers from the past who not only understood the difference between what we call technological and what we know as spiritual but also prepared us for the challenges of our times.

THE ERA OF AHRIMAN

Before we move on to the final part of our detective work, I would like to ask: Has there been anyone in modern times who, in one way or another, has warned us about the dangers of complying with the mechanical-logical way of seeing life, the Universe, and ourselves as being devoid of Spirit or higher form of consciousness?

It was nothing short of synchronicity that, as I was formulating my understanding of the concept of evil as a form of ignorance or the gross misconstruction of a materially oriented mind, I came across Rudolf Steiner's five public lectures from 1919. Until the moment when I became deeply involved in an inner dialogue with Simone, I had never read Steiner's work. As a spiritual detective, I had heard about him but had never studied him. As a student of esoteric teachings, I was aware of him, and as an academic, I knew of Steiner's schools but had never gone to any effort to research him, as I was too intently involved with esoteric Tantra and Gnosticism. For those who, like me, know him only as a name, Steiner (1861-1925) was a German esoteric teacher and theosophist. During his lifetime, his most-read book was *The Philosophy of Freedom*, first published in 1894. After his death, his work received more recognition in theosophical circles where his public lectures are discussed and are often seen as prophetic for our times.

One of the themes of Steiner's public lectures given in the first two weeks of November 1919 delved into the idea of Ahriman. Ahriman was not Steiner's invention. This figure was considered a demonic entity in the ancient Persian religion of Zoroastrianism. However, in his 1919 lectures, Steiner gave Ahriman a new status: as a new incarnation of evil. As I read through Steiner's lectures, I gathered that in his system of beliefs, Ahriman was the third incarnation of the "cosmic triad" that began first with the incarnation of Lucifer in the third millennium BCE in the East, then with Christ in the first century CE in the Middle East. He considered Ahriman as the final incarnation of the triad.

What was of interest to me, personally, was the way in which Steiner explains how the entity will prepare us for his arrival. This preparation, Steiner believed, began in the fifteenth century CE in the West, which initiated the dawn of materially conceptualized science through the discoveries of Galileo and Copernicus.

According to Steiner, this was when we lost our natural perception of the cosmos as spiritual and began focusing on the material aspects of the world. From then on, the cosmos began to be perceived as a "huge machine," with humanity forgetting that the cosmos was soulful and spiritual in nature. Steiner specifies two temptations within Ahriman's preparation of human minds for his arrival. The first one is the complete and unquestionable focus on the material aspects of the cosmos. I believe he meant that our focus will turn to mathematical calculations rather than deeper understanding. The second tempting is that all we need is material and economic welfare. Nowadays, we would call it "economic determinism," which is the conviction that if something is economically sound and creates material well-being, it is inherently good.

Steiner estimated that this will happen at the beginning of the third millennium. At this time, Ahriman will incarnate as a human. Our minds will be easily confused by his materialistic rhetoric and perceptions, because all we will know is matter and money. In other words, he will be incarnated because we will be completely brainwashed by worship of materially limited sciences and the prioritizing of economic well-being above everything else. Steiner does not leave us hopeless there. On the contrary, in his third and fourth lectures, he implores humanity to "confront Ahriman face to face."

And how do we do this? There are two ways to confront him. One is to become acutely alert of all the aspects of our lives that are affected by solely materialistic and economic aspects. The other way is to work on our own spiritual evolution. If humanity does not do these two things, then our whole culture will be permeated by Ahriman's agenda, and we will not even notice what he represents.

I find Steiner's lectures prophetic. He foresaw how we will be overwhelmed by the amount of contradictory information thrown at us, perhaps with the sheer purpose of confusing us so we will not be able to see through the Ahrimanic agenda. In short, humanity will be so polarized that it will be very easy for Ahriman and his materialistic values to infiltrate our lives without anyone even noticing. I think it is difficult to deny that this is a correct description of our current reality: economically, politically, and spiritually. This, in turn, allows for a naïve and reckless plunge into transhumanistic agendas and sophistry. Had Steiner been alive today, I am certain he would have seen transhumanist and post-humanist ideas as Ahrimanic.

In Pasulka's Encounters, Simone jokes that even her family thinks she is an AI from the future. I would not be surprised. There seems to be the intuitive but undeniable connection between the rise of AI technology and UFO phenomena. UFOs, whether seen as interdimensional events occurring in the numinous spaces between the waking and dream realities or as spaceship encounters, are somehow vested in human development, history, and future. I would even go so far as to say that "aliens" might be humans or AI technology from the future and are here to influence the trajectory of our history.

I am reluctant to put all UFO phenomena into the same category, as some researchers classify them as threatening and others see them as solely beneficial to us and friendly. Based on the narratives of experiencers, these encounters can seem either friendly or not, but in both kinds of encounters, the aliens are interested in conveying or even downloading compressed information to us. The esoteric traditions often refer to the struggle between the good and nefarious powers of the Universe.

Could they be referring to our otherworldly messengers and their intention for us?

Professor Gary Nolan of Stanford University has been a passionate proponent of the reality of UFO phenomena. In his interview with Ross Coulthard (2024), Nolan mentions that we could be facing a form of speciation. Speciation occurs when members of the same species, in our case humans, are separated from one another and diverge due to different circumstances and conditions that they have faced. As a result, they can end up as two separate species.

As I intimated in my vision at the end of Part 1 of this book: Are we now being contacted by two versions of ourselves competing to influence the trajectory of our development in one direction or another: one multidimensional and the other technological? Or is there a more basic distinction: one biological and the other either as a humanoid robot with some form of consciousness or a human-technological hybrid? Perhaps one of them is trying to warn us against merging with technology and the consequences of that choice while the other tempts us with advanced technology as a means of evolution. If this is so, are we facing two very different and competing realities of UFOs beckoning us from the future?

Yet hardly anyone even considers the possible reality of another form of wisdom, which is often represented mythologically as a goddess. In the same vein, many esoteric texts speak of the wisdom of the intuitive kind, all embracing and powerful, that takes us to the depths beyond the limits of our rational-logical minds. In both instances, Goddess represents the form of wisdom that dissolves the polarities of our mundane realities. She often appears from another place or dimension, whether as Inanna, who descends from the Great Above; Demeter, who comes down from Olympus to teach humanity higher perception; Mary Magdalene, who is the only disciple of Jesus capable of accessing the imaginal space of *nous*; or Sophia who, after being blinded by the false light, ascends again to higher levels of consciousness.

"I was sent forth from Power!" exclaims the Goddess of the Gnostic poem "Thunder, Perfect Mind" from the third century CE. "I'm the first and the last. I am the whore and the holy one... For I am knowledge and ignorance... Do not be ignorant of me... Give heed to me... Hear me, you hearers, and learn of my words, you who know me."[12]

Elaine Pagels, in *The Gnostic Gospels* (1989), quotes from another Gnostic text, *Trimorphic Protennoia*: "I am the real Voice... I cry out within everyone, and they know that a seed dwells within... It is I who speak within every creature... Now I have come a second time in the likeness of a female."[13]

As spiritual detectives, we need to ask: Will her voice be recognized, or will she be banished as an alien goddess? Let's continue our exploration.

PART 3
THE REVELATION:
THE GODDESSES OF ASCENSION

UNCOVERING GODDESS WISDOM

Entering the sacred space of Goddess wisdom is seldom a straight path. First, we have to acquaint ourselves with those who spoke against the Goddess.

When I was at the University of Toronto and at the Pontifical Institute, I was not a critical student. On the contrary, I was hungry for wisdom and accepted what I was told without any doubt. There is a good side to such unconditional commitment to learning without questioning what one is told, because it allows us to learn more and, in knowing more, we can then be open to seeing information differently. We can discover any hidden plots behind the stories that might have been forgotten or removed on purpose. This kind of detective work to uncover the lost wisdom requires the same devotion and the same commitment.

While an undergraduate and postgraduate student, I frequented a scholarly bookshop near the University of Toronto and, if I remember correctly, it was a part of that university. It was a spacious place, almost hangar-like, with books lying on the tables everywhere and with many bookshelves. I seldom looked at the books on the shelves and the tables, because the books I needed were never there. My interests were in ancient texts and their interpretations, and these kinds of books required a special order.

Often, I would go straight to the counter and ask a scholarly looking, bespectacled man or a woman whether they could order me this book or that. The bookkeepers at the counter looked at this young blonde woman with an Eastern European accent with friendly curiosity. There was almost a protective spark in their eyes, and surprise that someone like that still existed with such hunger to know things long discarded as irrelevant in the world of the fast and easy. They always told me that, no problem, they could order the books I was seeking.

On one occasion, my order was for the *City of God* by the fourth-century saint, Saint Augustine. This was the very book that the priest professor at the Pontifical Institute had told me nobody read anymore, and just as well, as it ridiculed goddess rituals as abominations!

Now, decades later, people often ask me about initiations and practical rituals. Once I received a review complaining that one of my books had beautiful stories and theories, but that the reader wanted something practical. Ah! There is no deeper path, there is no more sacred initiation than devotional plunging into the wisdom of esoteric texts. This is not an easy journey. You can light candles if you want, but it is not about the candles or dressing up. It is an opening of your own mind to the higher wisdom that the sacred texts of the past carry.

Don't be discouraged, although the reading is not easy. Know that this wisdom has many layers, and each layer is an invitation to go deeper. Some of us need to hear the story itself, the narrative, before we can progress further. And when ready, we can peel back all the other layers until the mystery speaks to us. So, I implore you to be patient with the Mysteries of the Goddess that I am opening for you now. They will initiate you. They will give you what you need on your path at this very moment.

The initiation journey begins with the unpeeling of the mysterious layers of *The Descent of Inanna* in the lands of ancient Mesopotamia and Assyria. *The Descent of Inanna* is told in a strictly mythological way, as it is most likely the most ancient goddess stories. Perhaps the people for whom the story was told still remembered the hidden mystery behind it.

Next, we will move to the labyrinths of ancient Crete and investigate the secrets of the Eleusinian Mysteries and the *Homeric Hymn to Demeter*. The longest and most challenging climb in this process is the esoteric teaching of ascension from *The Gospel of Mary Magdalene* found in Egypt. The mystery teachings of *The Gospel of Mary Magdalene* are unique in the way that, unlike the previous sacred stories of the Goddess, they give us inner tools for the ascension process. Then we will move on to the story of Sophia, also found in Egypt, which is an encoded story of humanity as it is now. *Pistis Sophia* is a truly prophetic text as we dive into chapters 28 to 82 of this challenging, esoteric work.

The final unveiling or revelation comes from a very unusual source—Baba Yaga, the primal goddess before she was even known as a goddess—and her relationship with humanity. Reading these texts is a rewarding and thought-provoking process, as every true initiation is. I hope they will become a part of your sacred path and will initiate you, as they have initiated me.

Why do we need this invitation to the myths of goddesses?

Myth is a tricky word, and I usually avoid using it. Like the word *goddess*, it has been diluted and, therefore, stripped of its significance and power. Originally, *myth* comes from the ancient Greek word *mythos* which, in turn, means "word."

We need to remember that "word" was not just a word for ancient people; it was a pronouncement of power. In ancient magic, knowing the names of the gods, for example, gave us power over them. We could summon them, ask for assistance, and change our reality. As times have changed and the great magic of the word has been forgotten by some and misused by others, we have become unconscious creators. We speak words as if they have no meaning or power attached to them, and we create realities over which we believe we have no influence. But what if not everyone believes this, and if others, whoever they are, use words to create realities for us, realities that do not benefit our evolution—realities that aim to keep us at the lowest levels of our consciousness?

These are the reasons why I do not treat the sacred texts I have been speaking of as myths. I do not want them to be discredited as just tales. They are the original stories for us to remember and learn from. They teach us the reality of our descent to the lower realms through treachery, betrayals, or our own misunderstandings and delusions. They also give us very specific tools for how we can ascend and evolve.

The ascension process, according to the sacred texts, is an inner job. There is no other way. The friendly aliens might warn us when we stray again towards wrong understanding and devolution, but they can't save us. Only we can save ourselves through our inner work. Then, and only then, does Grace appear. We are alone on this journey, but first we need to be willing to undertake it. This willingness is a daily remembrance of our choices. Each movement of consciousness can lead us to descent or ascension, devolution or evolution.

The sacred texts describing both journeys are our first initiation.

GODDESS CONSCIOUSNESS TRAPPED: THE DESCENT OF INANNA

For millennia, endless traditions of Goddess lineages have celebrated another form of consciousness that embraced our humanness while accepting our inherent Divinity. In those traditions, our humanity was not separate from our Divinity; our bodies, our sexuality, and all of the natural world were accepted as pathways to transcendence and a deeper connection with the beingness of all creation. The traditions carried sacred knowledge of our part in the beautiful symphony of the cosmos. They showed us the very fabric of our existence. There was no separation between the mind and the heart, the soul and matter, humans and nature. Indeed, these concepts did not exist because the idea of separation did not exist. The very idea would be treated as a strange perversion of the cosmic order. We lived in the womb of the Goddess and existence was our playground.

That is precisely why, in our detective work, I would like to investigate the esoteric sources that discuss the mysteries of goddess traditions and Goddess Consciousness. Esoteric traditions are often passed on to us in the form of myths and poems that are open to many interpretations. Regardless of whether we look into ancient myths, religions, or classical Tantra, the texts are usually encoded. This is problematic, as these texts were written with the purpose of hiding their meaning from the uninitiated and revealing their truths to the initiated alone.

Unfortunately, most scholarly efforts belong to the uninitiated category and are limited to a very basic understanding of the sources they study. For this reason, they make little sense to anyone who does not know how to read them, and, because of this, both the myths and esoteric texts are delegated as curiosities at best or are treated as the made-up stories of less advanced civilizations. Even the most well-intentioned scholars, often through no fault of their own, read these esoteric texts at their most basic level. As a result, we have access to them, but we do not understand them.

Let's start our investigation with the myth of the Descent of the Goddess Inanna. We can't begin this journey without explaining the status of the Goddess in Sumerian culture as well as in alternative views on her place in human consciousness. In most ancient history books, the Goddess Inanna is described, more or less, in universal terms as the goddess of wisdom, war, justice, fertility, sensuality, Divine law, and political power. Archaeologists have found evidence of the worship of Inanna as far back as 4000 BCE in Sumer, a civilization which developed between the Euphrates and Tigris rivers. In later cultures she was also known as Ishtar and Astarte.

In my research, I have also uncovered her connection to the Egyptian Goddess Isis and, closer to our times, to Mary Magdalene, and I have argued that these goddesses represent a particular lineage that has been deleted from our collective memory. The archaeological findings provide us with tangible aspects of Inanna associated with her worship. Mythological sources place her as the Queen of Heaven belonging to a particular family of gods called *Anunnaki*. Inanna, as far as we know, is one the seven main Anunnaki who determine the "fate of humanity." Apart from Inanna, there are six other major Anunnaki: An, Ninhursag, Enlil, Enki, Nanna, and Utu.

The Anunnaki also have an interesting alternative narrative. The one that is most popular among some UFO circles is that described by Zacharia

Sitchin in his *Anunnaki Chronicles* (2015). Sitchin controversially claims that the Anunnaki are extraterrestrials from a planet called Nibiru. Although Sitchin's ideas are not easily digestible for me, many other researchers support at least some of his ideas and note that there might be more to the Anunnaki than just myth. Graham Hancock in *Fingertips of the Gods: The Evidence of Earth's Lost Civilization* (1995), for example, claims that the Anunnaki possessed superior technology when they first appeared in Sumer. Whoever the Anunnaki are in these narratives, for us, the key source of information on Inanna is the poem *The Descent of Inanna*—so let's focus on this primary source first.

The Descent of Inanna

The Descent of Inanna was written between 1900 BCE and 1600 BCE but was known for much longer in oral traditions. *The Descent of Inanna* stands on its own, but many traditional scholars like to refer it back to the Epic of Gilgamesh. I find it both curious and suspicious that the dates for the Epic are estimated as being between 2100 and 1200 BCE. In my research, dating works is often done in line with attempts to demean the importance of goddess-related literature. If the *Epic of Gilgamesh* was created in the year 2100 BCE, this would place the Epic as preceding *The Descent of Inanna*.

I find it much more likely that the two stories are either contemporary to one other or that *The Descent of Inanna* is the older text. I think the placement of the *Epic of Gilgamesh* before *The Descent of Inanna* may have been an attempt to explain the reason behind Inanna's descent and forcing this into one particular narrative about her, which I explain below. But back to the main plot of Inanna's descent. I would like us to read this story as if it were a child's tale at first and then to analyze it more deeply. We will focus now on the most basic storyline of the poem.

The Goddess Inanna decides to descend from the sky to visit her sister, who lives in the Underworld. Inanna knows her sister is preparing the funeral rites for her husband, the Bull of Heaven. Inanna takes her faithful servant Ninshubur with her but asks her to stay outside the gates of the Underworld. She instructs her servant that if she does not return, Ninshubur must go to the other Anunnaki gods and ask them to send help.

As Inanna enters the Underworld, she is ordered by the gatekeeper to remove the symbols of her power at each of the seven gates leading to the chamber in which her sister mourns her husband. Reluctantly, Inanna agrees, as the gatekeeper tells her these are the rules of the Underworld. At the seventh and last gate, Inanna is only a shadow of her former self and is completely at the mercy of her sister and her judges. The judges decide that Inanna must be put to death, and she is killed. Her body is left hanging to rot for three days.

In the meantime, Inanna's servant, seeing she has not returned, makes the rounds of the other Anunnaki gods, but only one of them agrees to help her. This god, Enki, sends two tiny beings as small as flies, with instructions to distract Inanna's sister with their compassion so she will then agree to release Inanna's rotting body. This is precisely what happens, and the two tiny beings subsequently manage to revive Inanna through magic. However, before Inanna can leave, she has to promise that she will send someone to take her place in the Underworld.

Inanna has no choice in the matter but does not want to sacrifice her sons, so she has to find someone else to replace her. When she returns to her heavenly dwelling, she finds out that in her absence, her lover Dumuzi has taken her throne and therefore betrayed her. Inanna decides to sacrifice him as punishment for the betrayal. In the end though, he is required to spend only six months of the year in the Underworld, and for the other six months, he can enjoy being Inanna's consort.

Before we plunge into our own detective work, I would like to honor the traditional academic and modern take on the myth. The traditional academic interpretations are not friendly towards the Goddess Inanna. This does not surprise me one bit. In my book *The Other Goddess*, I elaborate on how nearly all female-oriented narratives, either in myths or in sacred texts, are interpreted in a way that either discredits the female protagonist or makes a villain out of her—and when this is not possible, the interpretations turn her into a prostitute.

The story of Mary Magdalene is the classic case of this approach. Traditional academics have treated Inanna as a villain and a seductress with a history of choosing her men or other gods as lovers, a crime some old professors could not forgive. In fact, according to some old academic conclusions, Inanna's is a story of injustice. How dare she get what she wants and not be punished for this? This is a very Victorian attitude. Inanna's own love and erotic choices only add to her allure, in my opinion.

In more recent times, *The Descent of Inanna* has been interpreted as Inanna literally coming down into the Underworld, which means the world of the dead in either the literal or psychological sense. Proponents of the modern psychological tradition have started to interpret this as a story of the *psyche* coming into wholeness. In Jungian terms, Inanna and her sister, as well as Inanna's lover, are one and the same person. They are seen as playing different parts or aspects of the ego. Jungian psychoanalysis views this as a story of integrating our shadow into the oneness of our personality.

Similarly, feminist interpretations tell her story from the point of view of the archetype of a strong goddess going through complete transformation, facing her fears, and coming back to Earth. All of these interpretations are meaningful and important. The reason we are not looking more deeply into them here is because there have been many good books written about this already. I would especially like to recommend *The Way of Inanna* (2022) by Seana Zelazo. *The Way of Inanna*, for me, is the touching story of coming to wholeness through facing one's own shadows and through forgiveness, all of which is beautifully supplemented by Zelazo's own story of healing after traumatic experiences in her life.

The Descent of Inanna is so steeped in symbolism that it is an immense task to interpret it. Many different people at different times, especially in modern times—have interpreted it in various ways. But I think it is important to look at the poem itself so we can fully understand the hidden meaning behind *The Descent of Inanna*. Why do I think it is important to do this? Because it is the way the people who remembered *The Descent of Inanna* wrote and described it. Only then can we know what truth they wanted to pass on to future generations and what they wanted us to learn, both about them and our own past.

The best way of deciphering the meaning of the myth is to go to the original text. I have always found it a great privilege to be able to look at the original text, and although translations inevitably create a barrier of meaning as the simple choice of words in translation can alter the message of the original, they also give us as much immediate access to the story as is humanly possible. In order to more closely read *The Descent of Inanna*, I have chosen the translation by Diane Wolkstein and Samuel Kramer.

In our detective journey, I would like us to consider that *The Descent of Inanna* tells the story of her descent from a higher level of consciousness to a lower level of consciousness. I would like to propose that the point of origin in the story is not the ego and is not the Earth. In arguing this case, we have to go through the poem with a fine-tooth comb looking for hidden clues. I think it is important to start with the beginning of the poem, because this is how the ancients chose to start it. It is also the beginning of the poem that gives us the right clues we are setting out to discover.

I would like us to pay close attention to the opening three lines of the poem. The first line is: "Goddess Inanna *from the Great Above* gave her ear to the Great Below." This is repeated three times. This often omitted line is essential if we want to interpret the hidden meaning of the myth. Why is this repetition in the first lines of the poem important? I do not believe that the "Great Above" refers to the Earth, as the Earth is not above us. And the

120

"Great Above" cannot refer to the state of the ego, as the ego is neither higher than us nor is it far from us. Modern interpretations seem to ignore this point in the origin of Inanna's journey.

Pinpointing the precise place of departure in Inanna's story is significant because it tells us Inanna was going to descend from heavenly levels rather than from the Earth. In our mythological exploration, this changes the perspective completely. Inanna is not descending from her ego to her subconscious—these concepts did not exist at that time—but from the higher realms (the heavens?) to the lower, earthly realm. In other words, this is a story of stepping down from either a higher dimension or from the physical sky (the Great Above).

This changes the plane from which the Goddess Inanna starts her journey. This also changes the perspective from which the myth is written— by people who observed her descent and therefore were either dimensionally or geographically lower than the Goddess. This could symbolize the "heavens versus Earth."

It is also important to remember that the Goddess chose to do this of her own volition; that is, no one forced her or asked her to do this. This element of the myth, as we will later learn, corresponds to other mythical accounts from different times and cultures. Inanna "gave her ear to the Great Below," which means that she had heard something from the lower realms (at least lower to her own usual realm) and chose either to explore this or to answer the call coming from "the Great Below."

It appears that Inanna was aware of the possible dangers in her descent, as she does two things before she begins: She "gathers the seven *me*" with her, and she orders her faithful servant Ninshubur to go with her. The *me* here can be interpreted in a couple of ways: either as the Goddess' magical powers or, in a more mundane manner that traditionalist scholars prefer, as "the essential laws and offices of civilization derived from Divine order found in the primordial mother Nammu." This second definition of *me* comes from

The Oxford Companion to World Mythology and it was a nice surprise to see that they acknowledge the primordial and Divine origin of the *me*, even if this definition does not acknowledge the magical and protective powers of the *me*, which are repeated in many goddess-centered mythologies.

Ninshubur is often overlooked in interpretations, but she is one of the most important characters in the story. She symbolizes Inanna's memory of her greatness, of her original belonging to the higher realms—the realm of Higher Consciousness or what in New Age parlance is called the "higher self." It is no coincidence that it was Ninshubur in whom Inanna confides when she descends from the sky to the realms below the sky. She tells her servant that she might not come back and says that if she does not return, Ninshubur must mourn for her, must beat the drums for her "in the assembly houses," and must "circle the houses of the gods" to tell them that she has not come back from the Underworld.

She orders her to go to three Anunnaki gods. The first is the God Enlil, the God of the Sky. Ninshubur must ask him to help Inanna. If he refuses to help the Goddess, then Ninshubur should go to the God Nanna, who is the God of the Moon, and ask him to help her. If help does not come from Nanna, Ninshubur must appeal to the God Enki, who is the God of Earth and Wisdom, and ask him to help her.

When Inanna and Ninshubur arrive at the Great Below, Inanna, knowing the danger of the situation and aware that she must go through this ordeal alone, asks Ninshubur to leave her. And there, at the gates of the Great Below, she meets Nethi, who is the gatekeeper of the Underworld. Nethi represents the separation between the realms of higher and lower consciousness. Once Inanna faces Nethi, she will enter another realm in which different rules, thinking, and behavior apply.

Nethi the gatekeeper is surprised to see her and asks: "What are you doing here, Goddess Inanna?" to which she answers, "I have come to see my sister Ereshkigal because her husband the Heavenly Bull has died. So I have come for his funeral rites."

Nethi then goes to Inanna's sister, Ereshkigal, and tells her (I am simplifying the language here), "Look, this powerful goddess is at the gates. She says she wants to come in and she is wearing the crown, she wears beads, she wears chest plates, she has a wonderful ring, and she's in beautiful robes. Should I let her in?" Ereshkigal thinks about this for a moment and then tells Nethi, "You know what? Let the magnificent Inanna in, but at each gate she must give up something, an essential part of herself." Therefore, so the myth goes, the higher consciousness is gradually given up, piece by piece, through descending to the lower realms.

Various versions of *The Descent of Inanna* mention different garments representing her abilities and mastery in the upper realm that she must give up. They usually include her crown, the beads around her face and neck, a breastplate, a ring, a scepter, a belt (girdle), and her royal robes.

For example, at the first gate, she has to give up her crown, which symbolizes the higher wisdom without which she is left with only a materially focused mind. At the second and third gates, she has to give up the beads around her face and neck. I believe they symbolize her ability of higher speech, which is her ability to perform magic and affect reality and its matrix. At the fourth gate, Inanna is asked to remove her breastplate, which leaves her heart unprotected. As a consequence, she loses the ability to see through the wisdom of the heart and to love unconditionally. At the fifth gate, depending on a version of the myth used, she has to give up either her scepter or her golden ring, which represents her power to rule justly. At the sixth gate, she needs to relinquish the girdle on her hips that adorns and represents her femininity. At the seventh and last gate, she is asked to give up her robes, which I believe are her heavenly body.

And then she is finally admitted to the Great Below, having been stripped of all of her Divine powers—including her Divine wisdom.

An alternative interpretation of the seven gates makes a connection between the gates and the chakra system in the Hindu tradition. This is an interesting possibility, and I would like to offer yet another interpretation.

1. Crown – Crown Chakra (Sahasrara)
    The crown symbolizes Divine authority, which can be aligned with the Crown Chakra, associated with higher consciousness and enlightenment. By giving up her crown, Inanna is surrendering her connection to the Divine and the upper realms.

2. Earrings and other head jewels – Third Eye Chakra (Ajna)
    The head adornments represent clarity of vision, insight, and perception, all qualities of the Third Eye Chakra. Removing them signifies letting go of intuitive sight, mental clarity, and discernment, leading Inanna to descend into a place of lower consciousness.

3. Necklace of Beads – Throat Chakra (Vishuddha)
    The necklace can be aligned with the Throat Chakra, which governs the ability to create through speech. As she removes her necklace, Inanna symbolically surrenders her ability to express herself.

4. Breastplate (Rod of Power) – Heart Chakra (Anahata)
    The breastplate, worn over the chest, can connect to the Heart Chakra, which represents pure love. Giving up her breastplate represents descending into confusing emotions and passions.

5. Scepter or Golden Ring – Solar Plexus Chakra (Manipura)
    The Solar Plexus Chakra is associated with both Divine will and personal will, the power to rule over others and the power to evolve. Removing her scepter or ring symbolizes a surrender of Inanna's authority, and submission to forces beyond her control, such as fate and death.

6. Girdle or Belt – Sacral Chakra (Svadhisthana)
    The girdle or belt, often interpreted as a symbol of sexuality and creativity, aligns with the Sacral Chakra, which governs sexual energy and allure.

By removing her girdle, Inanna surrenders her creative power, sexual identity, and the energy that fuels creation and pleasure.

7. Ankle Bracelets or Final Garment – Root Chakra (Muladhara)

The removal of her final garment or ankle bracelets leaves her fully naked. It represents the stripping away of all worldly attachments, including her physical security and identity. This can be aligned with the Root Chakra, which is concerned with survival, grounding, and the material world. By now, Inanna is a lost individual with no grounding in higher reality.

Whichever interpretation appeals to you, they all speak of a loss of wisdom, power, and the memory of who we are. When Inanna, once the Goddess of Heaven and Earth, is finally admitted to the Great Below and its lower realms, not only has she no recollection of who she is, but she is forced to stand in front of the *Anunna*—the judges living in the lower realm—so they can pass judgment on her. They decide that she must die because she should not have descended to the Great Below. Her sister Ereshkigal casts the eye of death on Inanna and Inanna dies. Her rotting body is left hanging on a hook in the Underworld.

When, after three days, Inanna has not come back, her faithful servant Ninshubur starts beating the drums because she is the last vestige of Inanna's memory of who she really is and wants to awaken the world to the loss of Inanna.

After beating the drums of her memory, Ninshubur visits the God Enlil and says, "God Enlil, please help your daughter Inanna because she is now dead in the Great Below." But Enlil is unwilling to help, believing that Inanna has brought death upon herself. She knew she should not descend from the higher to the lower realms and yet decided to do so.

Ninshubur then goes to the God Nanna, but he is also unwilling to give his assistance, because he believes that no one who has descended to the lower realms can ever return.

Finally, Ninshubur appeals to the God Enki who is "troubled" and "grieved" by what has happened. To help Inanna, Enki decides to resort to magic by creating two genderless beings: one called Kurgarra and the other Galatur. He makes them as small as flies so they can enter the Underworld unnoticed. To further assist them in the task of saving Inanna, he gives them "the food of life and the water of life" and orders them to go to the Great Below. He instructs them to wail along with Erishkigal at the funeral rites of her husband and to wait until she offers them a reward for their sympathy for her pain.

Kurgarra and Galatur do as they are told, and everything happens as Enki predicts. They receive the body of Inanna and sprinkle the food of life and the water of life on her body, which brings Inanna back to life. The magic of Enki works!

Although Inanna is now alive and is allowed to pass through all the gates of the Underworld, there is another obstacle. Suddenly, seven demons called *galla*—who pretend to have real powers but, in fact, are only demonic imposters—stop Inanna, Kurgarra, and Galatur and tell them that they cannot leave the Underworld unless Inanna sacrifices someone else in her place. Unaware that the demons are not who they claim to be, Inanna is forced to agree. The demons follow her through all the gates and then at the exit gate, they see Ninshubur. They ask if they can take her. But Inanna does not allow them to take her faithful servant, as she is Inanna's memory of her true identity.

Then the demons attempt to take her sons, Shara and Lula. Again, Inanna does not let them do so. The demons follow her to her palace, where Inanna sees her beloved, Dumuzi. But her beloved is not mourning for her. On the contrary, he has assumed her power and now sits on her throne. Outraged by his betrayal, Inanna decides to sacrifice Dumuzi to the demons of the Underworld in exchange for her freedom. He will have to go to the Great Below so that Inanna can remain in the Great Above.

Dumuzi has his own story where, after some adventures, he eventually has to spend six months of every year in the Underworld before returning to the Great Above for another six months.

Since this is such a fundamental story explaining our current place in the order of the Universe, it might be useful to remind ourselves of the main players in the myth and their symbolic meanings, wherever it is possible to decipher this. It might also be helpful to get used to the Sumerian names and the setting. Please note that this is my interpretation of the myth; there are many others, as I have mentioned earlier.

The Setting

The *Great Above* and the *Great Below* (which represent the higher and lower levels of consciousness)

The Great Above — The Main Players

Goddess Inanna, representing our wholeness when we have access to a higher level of consciousness, which is normally situated in the Great Above.

Ninshubur, Inanna's faithful female servant, who represents the memory of our state when we had access to the higher dimensions of consciousness.

Dumuzi, Inanna's lover who assumes her power when she is gone and is sacrificed in her place. He symbolizes something Inanna loves but needs to sacrifice to return to the higher realms.

The Anunnaki Gods

Enlil, the God of the Sky

Nanna, the God of the Moon

Enki, the God of Earth and Wisdom

The Great Below — The Underworld: Main Players

Nethi the gatekeeper, who lets Inanna know she must obey new rules when she descends to the Great Below.

Erishkigal, Inanna's grieving sister and the Goddess/ruler of the Great Below

Bull of Heaven, Erishkigal's dead husband, whom she mourns.

The Anunna, the judges who decide Inanna's fate when she reaches the Great Below, from which there is no return. Once you are there, there is no way out.

The seven gates through which Inanna needs to pass force her give up all memory of herself as a Divine being. This memory is represented by a crown, beads around the neck, beads on her chest, her breastplate, her ring, her scepter/measuring rod, and her robe—with some variations on her adornments in different interpretations.

Plot Details

Erishkigal casts the *eye of death* on Inanna after the judgement of the Anunna. Inanna's body is left for *three days* as rotting meat.

Ninshubur starts *beating the drums* to remind us about Inanna and begins the tour of the gods. She visits Enlil, Nanna and Enki.

The God Enki creates *Kurgarra and Galatur*, the tiny beings, and gives them *the food and water of life* to save Inanna.

Kurgarra and Galatur go to the Great Below and *wail with Erishkigal.*

Erishkigal gives them the body of Inanna, and they sprinkle it with the food and water of life which brings her back to life.

Seven Galla are imposter demons and deceivers who demand an exchange for Inanna.

In this detective journey, through the myth of Inanna, I have concluded that the myth represents the journey of humanity, which is both individual and collective. Originally, as with many myths, we have unlimited access to the Source. In fact, we are a part of the Divine order of the Universe. But something happened, possibly the movement of free will, curiosity, or some other mysterious reason—which led us to decide to descend to the lower realm of being.

In the interpretation I offer here, the Great Above is the evolved form of consciousness that has no sense of separation or division, when we are one with Source. Then the descent begins, and we learn that new rules apply in the lower realm. Through the process of descent, we not only lose our sense of Divinity and connection with all the cosmos, but we also lose the memory of our Divinity. We are now helpless and easily manipulated by strange rules and demonic imposters.

Most important of all, after we have descended, we either die or believe that we are finite, mortal beings composed only of physical existence and know only the material aspects of the world in which we live. We have completely lost our memory of who we are. We are nothing but rotting meat—or so we believe.

However, not all is lost because, when we embarked on this strange adventure of descent, we left behind a faint memory of who we truly are. This memory, which did not descend with us to the lower realm of being, is our true servant and our ultimate savior. It won't allow us or the world to forget our former glory, even if we are now debilitated. The story of Ninshubur, the faithful servant, is the centerpiece of the myth as it represents the moment of awakening and the sudden flash of memory that we are not just a powerless piece of rotting meat!

Ninshubur is the intuitive knowing that we are truly powerful and magnificent, even if we have been told otherwise by the rulers of the lower realm. We are correct in our intuition of our former glory, which we are now ready to reclaim. Ninshubur's journey to the realms of gods is really our journey of turning to the higher spiritual realms and asking for assistance. We know that we are not alone and that there is help in another place, whether this is through our own higher knowing or through external help.

Kurgarra and Galatur, who are genderless (often angels or other messengers from other realms are described as such), are sent from the Great Above to assist us on our upward movement to ascension. Yet ascension is not as easy as we might think, as we are easily fooled by demonic imposters (the *galla*) and, yet again, we are asked to relinquish something to be able to return to the higher realm.

The *galla* in *The Descent of Inanna* are another overlooked element, but they are essential for the explanation of the current state of the human condition. The seven *galla* are the imposter demons and deceivers. They are deceivers because they do not possess the powers that they have convinced us they possess. These are the powers that want to control us and determine our fate for us.

In esoteric traditions, the outer world is the reflection of the inner world. Therefore, it is our own wrong thinking and misperceptions (such as "I am not worthy") that keep us captive in the lower realms of consciousness or the lower dimensions. It is our own forgetfulness of our greatness and of our own divinity that is reflected in the outer world and submits us to the deceivers in the outside world.

The good news is, there is a way to change this, but it happens only through our inner action of transforming how we think of ourselves. Once we start thinking of ourselves as reflections of the Divine Source on a temporary earthly journey, we become agents of our own worthiness and greatness. And once we accomplish this, the external deceivers (the *galla*) will lose their power over us. They will be defeated because we won't believe their lies anymore. What is even better is that the external deceivers will disappear from our lives and reality and we will proceed on our ascension journey. Why? Because this is how consciousness works.

I find it very interesting that on the journey of ascension we must give up something that we deeply cherish (such as Dumuzi) which, however, has completely betrayed us. In the end, we can keep a part of this cherished thing (Dumuzi is allowed to stay with Inanna for six months of the year). The question is: What is this cherished thing that has betrayed us, but which we can still enjoy, even if only in half measure? Is this the partial memory of our embodiment, of our earthly adventure? Or is it something deeper, as other myths tell us? Do we leave behind a part of our divinity in the lower realm to help the lower entities to evolve?

Now, to strengthen this argument, I would like to note that there are many stories like this in other mythologies. For example, in *The Gospel of Mary Magdalene,* we see exactly the same story but with a focus on the ascent of consciousness. Similarly, in the Gnostic work *Pistis Sophia,* the Goddess Sophia voluntarily descends from the Great Above and then, after some adventures and difficulties, ascends to her rightful place. But first, we need to look at another very similar and powerful myth: the Eleusinian Mysteries and the *Homeric Hymn to Demeter.*

THE LOST ELEUSINIAN MYSTERIES: HOMERIC HYMN TO DEMETER

According to Nicola Bizzi's book *Egypt and Eleusinian Mysteries* (2020), before we can even speak of the Eleusinian Mysteries, we need to open ourselves up to the idea of "Eleusinity." Bizzi defines *Eleusinity* as a form of pre-Greek civilization known as the Minoan Civilization or the Cretan Empire, which spread on Crete, the Cycladic Islands, the mainland of Greece, and the coastal areas of Asia Minor. Bizzi claims it is the oldest known European civilization, possibly predating Egypt.

Who were the Minoans? Ethnically, the Minoan people, as we can see on the frescoes from the palace in Knossos on Crete, were slim and athletic with long black curls and olive skin. Other academic sources, notably Stephanie Seiler (2013) from the University of Washington, confirm that the Minoans "shared the greatest percentage of their mitochondrial DNA (that part of our DNA that determines our ancestry) with European populations, especially those in northern and Western Europe."[14]

The earliest known settlement in Knossos is dated as far back as 6970–6590 BCE. Therefore, both Bizzi's claims about Eleusinity—that it was a very ancient civilization and that it was of European origin—seem to be confirmed. These claims are important to check before we consider his other ideas about the Eleusinian Mysteries.

According to traditional scholarship, this civilization collapsed around 1200 BCE for unknown reasons, although a volcanic eruption is provided as a possibility. Bizzi, however, believes the collapse was due to the invasion of warrior tribes around the year 1184 BCE, when what we now know as Greek civilization took over and destroyed the Minoan civilization. Incidentally, this timing coincides with the dating of the Trojan War described by Homer in *The Iliad*; the introduction of the Olympian gods, commonly known as the Ancient Greek gods; the introduction of patriarchal values; and the primacy of the reasoning/local mind over more intuitive and immediate forms of knowing.

I am willing to accept Bizzi's reasoning because other mythologists whom I greatly respect, such as Joseph Campbell, as well as the mother of goddess anthropology, Marija Gimbutas, have also spoken of the same invasion. It makes sense mythologically as, according to early myths, the Goddess Persephone was born after the Goddess Demeter was raped by Zeus-Hippius (horse). Mara Lynn Keller, in her essay "The myriad faces, marvelous powers, and theology of Greek goddesses" (2018), claims that this description of Zeus the Horse represents "a god of the Indo-European clans that came down through central Europe, with their horses."[15]

From our point of view, as we move closer to the Eleusinian Mysteries and their connection with Goddess Consciousness and its descent and ascent, it is interesting to note that the Minoan culture was matrilineal, that is, of female lineage, and that that civilization worshipped ancient beings, the Titans. The Titans predated the Greek gods and were eventually defeated by them, in the same way as the matriarchal Minoan culture was defeated by the Greek warrior tribes.

Of course, other theories may also be correct. Perhaps the Minoan civilization disappeared because of a combination of several factors such as natural disasters and invasions that happened roughly the same time. Another part of Bizzi's hypothesis is that the city of Troy represented the Minoan civilization in Asia Minor, and once it fell, together with Knossos on Crete, the secret rites of the Eleusinian Mysteries "were transferred" to the town of Eleusis on the Greek mainland.

This transfer happened in 1216 BCE, when tradition says that the Goddess Demeter arrived there in her human form and "instituted the sacred Mysteries, pronouncing the Speech of Revelation." Demeter arrived in Eleusis "seeking her daughter who had been kidnapped by the Olympic God Hades—upon the order of Zeus—to prevent her mission to redeem humanity."

Now, this is very interesting. Why? It postulates that Demeter actually arrived in Eleusis in person! Not as a metaphor, but as an immortal person of Titanic lineage. The second amazing thing about this claim is that it confirms my intuition that the Eleusinian Mysteries are a mythological retelling of the descent and ascent of consciousness in a very similar way to the myth of *The Descent of Inanna*. For the sake of clarity, when Bizzi speaks of the Olympian deities, he means the Greek gods, such as, Zeus, Athena, etc., who populated what we now consider Greek mythology. The Greek deities and the ancient Titans were in conflict with each other, in the same way as the Minoan culture was in conflict with the new "usurpers," the warrior tribes.

In this view, the Eleusinian Mysteries were the saved remains of the ancient Minoan rites and sacred knowledge. According to Bizzi, after the fall of the Minoans, Demeter herself "transferred" the knowledge of the rites to Eleusis. Therefore, the Eleusinian Mysteries are really Minoan Mysteries, so to speak. In classical mythology, Demeter is considered as one of the Olympian gods, but throughout his book, Bizzi refers to her as a Titanic or Cyclonic goddess. Presumably, he does this based on the knowledge of her mission of saving the Mysteries and reestablishing them later in Eleusis.

The conquering warrior tribes knew nothing, or very little, of the higher Minoan culture that they had destroyed. I remember how shocked I was when I went to the ruins of Knossos while at an academic conference on Crete and learned that the Greek myths of Knossos were creations of the later Greek civilization. The Greeks tried to make sense of the mysterious Minoan civilization, and they did the best they knew how through the art of storytelling. One attempt at this was the famous Greek myth that supposedly took place in Knossos: the myth of Theseus and Ariadne.

In the myth, Theseus, an Athenian prince, is one of a group of seven young men and maidens who are selected every nine years to be sent to Crete to be eaten by a terrifying Minotaur in the labyrinth at Knossos. Princess Ariadne of Knossos falls in love with Theseus. She tells him to use a thread so he will not become lost in the labyrinth and be at the mercy of the terrible Minotaur, a human with the head and tail of a bull. The heroic Theseus does just this. He slaughters the Minotaur, then finds his way back out of the labyrinth by following the thread that Ariadne has given him.

I have always loved this myth, but it was only when I was in Knossos that I learned the myth was constructed after the fall of the Minoan civilization! What the Greek warriors saw was the labyrinthine ruins of the palace at Knossos with its beautiful images of the Minoan people performing acrobatic feats with bulls. Based on the complicated outlines of the palace and the paintings on its walls, the Greek warriors created their own explanations for the presence of the ruins. Interestingly, even that later myth suggests a power struggle between the Greek city of Athens and the Minoan civilization which, eventually, disappeared.

Once Minoan culture in Crete was destroyed, Eleusis became the "Mother Sanctuary" of the Mysteries as Demeter had ordered. And from there, Bizzi says, the temples "radiated" to other parts of the ancient world. He breaks down the development of the Mysteries into separate historical periods. For our detective work, it is enough to know only some of them. The first period occurred before Demeter's arrival in Eleusis. The second transpired from the time of Demeter's arrival in Eleusis in 1216 BCE until 780 BCE and established the rites of the Mysteries in the Eleusinian temple. The third and middle stage came about between 780 BCE to 360 BCE, and this enabled the spread of the knowledge of the Mysteries to the initiated and to the Greek mainland, Sicily, and North Africa.

The fourth stage (360 BCE to 50 CE) occurred when the Eleusinian Mysteries spread further to the Roman Empire, and the fifth stage (from 50 CE) marked the greatest expansion of the Mysteries, which continued until the destruction of the Eleusinian temples in 396 CE. Despite the spread of the Eleusinian Mysteries around the Mediterranean Sea, they proclaimed secret knowledge only to the initiated, who were bound to a vow of silence. They could not share the wisdom of the teachings of the Mysteries with others.

What were the Mysteries about? *The Encyclopedia Britannica* is neither very helpful nor very respectful in describing them, as it basically says, "Something was recited, something was revealed, and acts were performed, but there is no sure evidence of what the rites actually were, though some garbled information was given by later ..." However, the *Encyclopedia* tells us that the "Mysteries began with the march of the *mystai*, initiates, in solemn procession from Athens to Eleusis. The rites that they then performed in the Telesterion, or Hall of Initiation, were and remain a secret." We are also told that the rites included a ritual bath (a baptism?), three days of fasting (the number three again), and "completion of the still mysterious central rite." All of this was somehow connected with the afterlife.

Bizzi organizes what we know about the Mysteries a little better and adds two more features: the initiates shared salvation through the communion with the suffering fate and rebirth of the deities and the initiated were separated from the uninitiated as a community. The rites "ensured immortal life." He also confirms the absolute need to keep silent about what actually happened during the rituals. As in many of the Mystery traditions, the initiated were mentally freed from the societal system, as they had learned about the real meaning of reality. For pragmatic reasons, the initiated might still choose to follow the rules on which society was built, but they were aware that these societal rules were an artificial structure devoid of deeper meaning.

Many authors speculate about the actual rites, and I would like to caution everyone here. Having myself been initiated into a different esoteric tradition, I know that descriptions of rituals are often not helpful. The rituals by themselves are only steps or tools and are empty without the presence of a high initiate. Why? The high initiate her/himself acts as a conduit for the energy which s/he then passes to those who are invited to the initiation. But even the high initiate in the shape of a priestess, priest, guru, etc. is aware that they are there to invite the energy to be passed to others.

In my experience, without the aspect of the initiated one who can serve as a conduit, there is little use for any abstract knowledge of "how" or "what" to do. The high initiate gives the participants, future initiates, the experience of the energy, and only with that experience does absolute knowledge come. You know because you've experienced it. It is undeniable and you do not need to engage in any reasoning, as reasoning by itself proves nothing.

The other side of that experience is that no prior "believing" is necessary, only that there be trust in the process and openness to the experience. Once it is experienced, it is known. It cannot be known if it is not experienced. A vow of silence in most esoteric or mystery traditions might be just this truth: There is no point in describing what happens during the rites because either you have experienced this or you have not—that's it. Otherwise, the rites could be explained over and over again, but the uninitiated will still not understand what they are being told.

Imagine explaining the moment of falling in love to someone who has never experienced it or even heard of it before. Or, for the sake of an argument, suppose you are trying to describe an anomalous experience—whether of a spiritual, multidimensional, or extraterrestrial nature—to someone who does not allow for this possibility. They may just think you've lost your mind and could spend your time better making more money.

Who in the ancient world not only knew of the existence of the Eleusinian Mysteries but was also initiated into them? The short answer is, everyone who was anyone in the ancient world—but Bizzi scrupulously scans through the letters and works of ancient philosophers, poets, and even some emperors to prove his point. The initiates that are most known are Plato, Aristotle, Plotinus (Greek philosophers), Virgil (the author of the *Aeneid*), Cicero (a Roman philosopher, scholar, and statesman), and the Emperors Julian the Apostate and Marcus Aurelius (both were Roman emperors and renowned philosophers at the same time). There are many others. All of them wrote about the necessity of not sharing the Mysteries with the uninitiated. Plotinus—an influential Greek philosopher from the third century CE—stated this eloquently when he spoke about the "Mysteries of the two Goddesses":

> "This is the purport of that rule of our Mysteries: Nothing divulged to the Uninitiate; the Supreme is not to be made a common story, the holy things may not be uncovered to the stranger, to any that has not himself [sic] attained to see."

Therefore, the true meaning of the Eleusinian Mysteries, or any other Mystery teachings for that matter, were hidden in obscure language and mythological storytelling that had multiple meanings: a basic, external meaning, such as the rites of fertility and a deeper, esoteric meaning pertaining to immortality, the passage between life and death, and the ascent of human consciousness.

Homeric Hymn to Demeter

Let's go back to some primary sources so we are not simply relying on other people's opinions about them. One of the primary sources related to the Eleusinian Mysteries is the *Homeric Hymn to Demeter*. As with many ancient texts, this hymn is much older than its dating, as the sacred text and stories were preserved in oral form before they were written down. Scholars agree that this particular hymn was written down between 650-550 BCE. Most likely it was transcribed by an unknown bard, and it should not be confused with the epic works of Homer, the author of the *Iliad* and the *Odyssey*. We are told that the word "Homeric" refers not to a work's authorship but rather to the way in which a poem was written. There are thirty-three Homeric hymns that we know of, each dedicated to a particular deity and written roughly around the same time as Homer's epics as well as being in the same dialect and meter.

For our purposes, I am using a translation of the *Homeric Hymn to Demeter* by E. Evelyn White. I think it very useful to reimagine the hymn from the point of view of much more ancient esoteric traditions rather than via more recent interpretations related to the cyclical nature of time, agriculture, and the position of women on society. All the interpretations, although legitimate, do not take into consideration the esoteric meaning of the myth encapsulated in the hymn itself. It will also be helpful to simplify the plot of the story, as many mythological references which were obvious to Homer's contemporaries are not apparent to the modern reader. Once we accept that the hymn has an esoteric message to humanity, we can clearly see it is a way of telling us about the state of our consciousness and the lost freedom of humanity.

Before we can follow this story further and focus on its esoteric meaning, we need to familiarize ourselves with Hades' and Zeus' background stories. For this, we need to consider some aspects of the genealogy of the Greek gods and the Titans who preceded them. Their relationships were often incestuous, as offspring produced by sisters and brothers populate Greek myths. For our detective work, it is sufficient to know that all characters involved in the *Homeric Hymn to Demeter* are interrelated. Demeter herself, Hades, and Zeus were the children of Cronos—the god of Time. Cronos was the first real ruler of the world after he castrated his father Uranus, the god of Sky. Cronos was later killed by his son, Zeus, who replaced him as the ruler of the Earth.

From an esoteric point of view, it is important to note that all the characters of the *Homeric Hymn to Demeter* are already trapped in time, as they are the children of Time (Cronos). They are, however, still immortal and powerful. But since Cronos was born out of a union between the god of Sky and Gaea, everyone—including existing deities such as Demeter, Zeus, and Hades—henceforth lived in time and not in eternity. Somehow the union of the Sky and Earth created the dimension of time. Perhaps this limitation by time and the fall from eternity was the reason the god of Sky hated his children, especially Cronos.

There is a clear delineation between the Titans and the gods. Although Demeter, Hades, and Zeus are supposed to be children of the ancient Titans, they are not Titans themselves. They are somehow lesser than their parents and they need to eliminate the Titans to be the rulers of the Earth. This distinction between the Titans and the Olympic gods is very important, because the Eleusinian Mysteries brought back the ancient knowledge of how to exit time or at least gain immortality. This was known by Demeter, who was somehow more connected to her Titanic lineage than her siblings.

But back to the main story. The Goddess Persephone, Demeter's daughter, is snatched into the Underworld by the god of the Underworld, with the permission of Zeus who rules over other gods. Demeter, distraught that she cannot find her daughter anywhere, asks for assistance from other gods. First, she consults with Hecate, the goddess of magic. Hecate tells Demeter that she heard Persephone's desperate cry as she was being kidnapped but she cannot tell her who took Persephone away.

Hecate and Demeter then consult with Helios, the Sun god. Helios confesses to them that Persephone was taken away by Hades and taken into the Underworld on the orders of Zeus. Helios tries to console Demeter by telling her that the god of the Underworld is not such a bad match for her daughter, as he is born "out of the same stock." Now furious, Demeter roams the Earth in grief until she comes to rest at a place called the Maiden Well. There, earthly women find her but do not recognize her as a goddess because of her grief. They offer her a job—to look after the male infant of a local woman, which Demeter accepts.

Here is an important mention of Demeter's magical power of granting immortality. At night, when nobody is around, she buries the boy she is taking care of "deep into fire" to make him "deathless and unageing." However, the boy's mother, who does not understand the goddess' magic, snatches her baby out of the fire. Demeter, enraged that her rites of immortality have been interrupted, shows herself to the humans in her goddess attire and calls them "witless" and "dull mortals" who have prevented her from imparting immortality on the little boy.

Now visible to them as the Goddess Demeter, she orders them to build "a great temple and an altar … beneath the city" of Eleusis where she "will teach her rites which they will need to perform in her name to gain her favor." The people of Eleusis do as she asks and build her a "fragrant temple" with an altar.

Yet Demeter's grief at the loss of Persephone does not dissipate and she punishes the Earth with a "cruel famine" and "robs the gods" of their joy. Zeus attempts to console Demeter by sending her abundant gifts, but nothing can be a worthy substitute for Persephone. In the end, Zeus has no choice but to ask Hermes, the Messenger of the gods, to go to the Underworld and convince the god of the Underworld to give up Persephone. Hermes manages to do so but does not notice that Hades secretly put the seed of a pomegranate into Persephone's mouth. Persephone now reunites with her mother in a joyous embrace, but Demeter senses "some snare" and asks her daughter if she has eaten anything in the Underworld. She learns that Hades has fed her daughter the seed of a pomegranate, which binds her to him forever.

Eventually, Zeus and Demeter compromise: Persephone spends one-third of the year with the God of the Underworld, as his wife, but she returns to her mother for the other two-thirds of each year. Demeter immediately ends the famine and goes to her temple in Eleusis where she shows the people how to conduct her rites and "teaches them all her mysteries."

For us, the most instructive line of the hymn is at the line at the end (II.470-482): "Happy is he among men upon earth who has seen these mysteries; but he who is uninitiate and who has no part in them, never has lot of like good things once he is dead, down into the darkness and gloom."

After teaching the rituals, Demeter agrees to return to Olympus to live there with the other gods and goddesses.

In summarizing the plot of the *Homeric Hymn to Demeter,* I occasionally hint at the mystical meanings of some of the symbolism in the story. Now let's look at the hymn as closely as possible to discern its intended esoteric teachings without having been initiated to this particular tradition. If we agree with my premise that myths have an encoded message for humanity and speak of the same story of the descent and ascent of consciousness, decoding them is not only our obligation but an action necessary for our highest good.

The first line of each Homeric hymn and of each mythological storytelling is extremely important. The *Homeric Hymn to Demeter* opens with the line: "I will sing of the rich-haired Demeter ... and her trim-ankled daughter" who, by the order of Zeus, was given to Hades, the son of Cronos. This sounds like a typical opening of a Greek myth, but it is so much more.

Now let's decipher the line "Demeter is the goddess who taught humanity the Eleusinian Mysteries." Her daughter, Persephone, symbolizes someone or something the Goddess prizes most. This highly prized thing is snatched away by the lord of lower consciousness with the help of a new god who usurps the ancient powers. Thus, the Goddess' most precious possession is taken away from her by the alliance of the god of the lower consciousness (the Underworld) and the usurping god.

The mother-daughter myth in the *Homeric Hymn to Demeter* is especially touching, as almost everyone can relate to the emotional truth of the story. Mother and daughter were once one—not only one body of creation but also of one consciousness, one Source. Then something, some kind of trick, some innocent action, such as Persephone reaching out for a beautiful, radiant flower, was turned into a tragedy that affected the whole of humanity. As the god of lower consciousness takes her away to where she cannot be found, she is lost to her mother. What follows affects not only humans, not only the Earth, but the gods as well, as something is irreversibly lost, some knowledge is hidden from us.

In my interpretation, Mother-Daughter represents the unifying consciousness, as it was at the moment of Creation. The abduction of the daughter, Persephone, represents the abrupt separation and disruption of the original oneness. In other words, a part of the original consciousness descends into the lower realms represented by the Underworld.

As we also see through other similar stories, this descent was not intended. It was either an error of judgment, a temporary infatuation represented by the unusual beauty of the flower, or a trick by some other calculating power—Zeus, in this case. But what is done is done and now a part of our consciousness is banished from us. The great loss of this part of ourselves, which I would call our Divine heritage, is represented by Demeter's grief. However, Demeter is the key in this story of salvation of our return to unity consciousness, as she is the one who remembers her beautiful daughter and feels her loss. Nothing makes sense without her. Demeter is the memory of unity consciousness, the original state of humanity endowed with Divine qualities and understanding. It is she who does not give up on her daughter and who relentlessly seeks help.

In every good story, several helpers appear to assist the protagonist. First it is Hecate, who represents magic. She, too, hears Persephone's cry as she is being abducted and she, too, is aware that she is missing. She performs the important role of confirming to Demeter that she is not crazy, that an important part of her is missing and needs to be found. Hecate can be a teacher or an insightful friend in our life who feels our sense of disconnectedness and she, too, understands, that something very valuable has been lost, even if everyone around you tells you that "things are not so bad." In the plot of the myth, everyone telling Demeter that the God of the Underworld is not a bad match for her daughter represents the collective thought of delusion. But Hecate knows this is not true and shares Demeter's sense of loss. She feels it, even if she cannot tell Demeter exactly what has happened.

Demeter's second helper is Helios, who is a Titan and not a god, and therefore is more ancient and has more insight into the situation. Helios has not only witnessed the abduction but also knows the reason for it. He tells them that there has been a secret agreement between Hades and Zeus—an agreement that was not shared with the goddesses—to sacrifice Persephone to the God of the Underworld. Therefore, a part of our consciousness has been snatched away from us without our consent. Both humanity and the goddesses have been tricked into the lower realms of consciousness.

Demeter, who represents the memory of a part of us that is lost, is furious at the gods' betrayal and refuses to join them at Olympus where they reside and rule over humanity. Demeter, or our memory of what we have lost, roams the earth until she arrives at the Maiden Well, which is another significant symbol. The Maiden Well in mythology represents both the gateway to the Underworld, guarded by maiden cupbearers, and rebirth by virtue of the well's virgin waters. It is often associated with the sacred feminine space which, once lost, might signify the loss of protection for humanity.

It is at the Maiden Well that Demeter meets local women who offer her help. What is interesting about the substory of the Maiden Well is that Demeter tells the women she has come there from Crete, and not by her own will, but also by abduction. The reason this subplot is significant is that, according to Bizzi (2020), the original Eleusinian Mysteries came from Knossos in Crete and were lost together with the ancient civilization on Crete who worshipped the Titans and not the gods.

The local women believe her story. Demeter gets a job caring for the male infant of a local family and attempts to perform the rites of immortality on him, possibly the Eleusinian Rites, but is interrupted by the ignorant mother who fears for her child's well-being and does not understand Demeter's intentions. This could suggest that there has been at least one failed attempt at reviving the lost part of our consciousness or at granting humanity immortality. But something has gone wrong, and we are still incomplete. The failed attempt at rebirth results in destruction and the suffering of both humanity and the gods.

Through her perseverance, the memory represented by Demeter of what we have lost, forces the gods who caused the loss, to bring that part back from the lower consciousness. However, a return to unity consciousness cannot happen without a sacrifice. Through the trickery of lower consciousness, we are forced to exist on both levels, just as Persephone must move between the two worlds. Yet the movement back to the unity consciousness and a higher dimension of being is not an automatic thing and is reserved only for the initiated—those with whom Demeter has shared her rites of rebirth.

In this myth, Demeter, as our memory that something has gone wrong and that we need to restore our rightful place in the Universe, is the key figure. Without that memory, we are forever lost in chaos and suffering.

The path is there for those who are willing to act on that memory through initiation to sacred mystery traditions.

As in the myth of Inanna, this is a story of the descent and ascent of consciousness. Even the characters are similar. Demeter, like Ninshubur, is the memory of the descent of consciousness into lower levels or dimensions; Persephone, like Inanna, is the lost part of our consciousness; Hades, the God of the Underworld, resembles Erishkigal; and there are gods who are summoned to help. Elements of the plot are repeated in crucial points of the story, such as grief at a loss and the trickery—or simple lack of concentration—that leads to the downfall or descent.

This trickery happens twice in both myths—once at the beginning when luring a goddess into the Underworld and once when a goddess is already in the Underworld. Then there is a partial sacrifice of the beloved and the assistance of magic when something out of the ordinary has to be procured to ascend again. Admittedly, the use of magic is lesser in the *Homeric Hymn of Demeter*, where it is represented by Hecate; in the myth of Inanna, magic is represented by the magical creations of the God Enki, Kurgarra, and Galatur.

An interesting aberration in the *Homeric Hymn to Demeter* is that the second manifestation of magic, after the eating of the pomegranate seeds, binds Persephone to the Underworld for part of the time. In the myth of Inanna, the second magical trick liberates her so she can return to the Great Above. However, in the myth of Inanna, the goddess is tricked again by the imposter demons (the *galla*) to give up her beloved Dumuzi.

If we go deeper into their stories, we might even see some similarities in these myths to the Anunnaki myth from Sumer. Indirectly, both myths refer to factions between gods and goddesses or entities who fight each other. In each of these stories, a goddess is somehow lost in the Underworld. In Inanna's case, the Goddess descended of her own volition. In the *Homeric Hymn to Demeter*, the Goddess' daughter, Persephone, is forcefully abducted and taken to the lower realms. In both myths, through the help of some gods/goddesses/entities, the Goddess is brought back either completely like Inanna or partially like Persephone.

In *The Other Goddess*, I asked myself who the goddesses were. Now I have come to the conclusion that they were and existed and perhaps continue to exist, as real entities. By "real," I mean they had a presence that could manifest in three-dimensional reality. They were powerful beings, or at least more powerful than humanity, and were interested in us. Their intentions are difficult to determine, as some of them were clearly trying to help us to evolve and felt protective towards us, while others just wanted to use us, manipulate us, or simply to be worshipped by us.

Why would they want to be worshipped by us? I think the desire to be worshipped goes beyond any self-serving vanity. Although, some gods were certainly vain and not particularly intelligent, they were interested in our attention and therefore our energy. Perhaps they were not that evolved spiritually, but they *knew* something we did not. They knew that to create and to flourish, they needed our attention.

So, this is all in the past, right? Not necessarily. If we continue to give these beings our energy and attention, nothing will change. Perhaps we do not call them gods anymore, but they still steal our attention and energy in one way or another. Let's consider this question: Why do some beings continually want to divert our attention to themselves, world events that might or might not happen, and the darker side of consciousness? Perhaps we are still giving them what they want, but under another name. Has the name of the game changed but not the rules? Whatever we think of them, they certainly were considered and seen as real by the ancients. And they certainly had their own wars and their own disputes to which they drew us in. It's not so very different really, is it?

The most important piece of information we have gathered through our detective journey into these two myths is that both have the same message: There is secret knowledge hidden in the stories of the descent and ascent. The descent represents the danger of staying in the lower level of consciousness which makes us vulnerable to manipulations from the powers at hand while the ascent represents the possibility of liberation to a higher level of consciousness through appeal to the supernatural forces of the Universe. The forces of the Universe are represented by benevolent goddesses and gods or other interdimensional or extraterrestrial beings.

Something interesting for the next part of our detective work is that the powers involved in human mythology can be either benevolent or self-serving. We will investigate how they relate to the Gnostic battle between good and evil as we look into *The Gospel of Mary Magdalene* and *Pistis Sophia*.

THE TOOLS FOR ASCENSION IN THE GOSPEL OF MARY MAGDALENE

T*he Gospel of Mary Magdalene* is the next sacred text in our detective journey. I have chosen to write about it after discussing *The Descent of Inanna* and the Eleusinian Mysteries, not only because of chronological reasons but also because of *The Gospel of Mary Magdalene*'s theme.

The Gospel of Mary Magdalene zooms in on the process of ascension, while the two previous traditions focus primarily on the descent and the magic needed to ascend. *The Gospel of Mary Magdalene* teaches us ascension techniques or, more precisely, how to ascend our consciousness, step by step. Out of all my investigative work, I have found this sacred text the most instructive. However, although it is instructive, that does not mean it is easy to practice or even to understand.

There is an ongoing discussion among scholars about the dating of *The Gospel of Mary Magdalene*, and to address some of their main points, we need to consider the story of its discovery. The first partial copy of the *Gospel* was found in 1896 in an antiquities shop in the city of Akhmim in Egypt, and it was purchased for the National Museum in Berlin. From now on, that particular partial copy of *The Gospel of Mary Magdalene* is known as the

"Berlin Codex." The Berlin Codex was written in Sahidic Coptic and was dated roughly to the fifth century CE.

Sometime between 1897 and 1906, two other copies of the *Gospel* were found, both written in Greek. These two Greek copies are known as the "Papyrus Oxyrhynchus," named after the city on the other side of the Nile from Akhmim, and the "Papyrus Rylands." The Greek versions were dated to at least the third century CE.

And now the battle of scholars begins. Those who believe that the first four Gospels in the Bible were the earliest written are very reluctant to consider any other Gospels which were not included in the Bible, insisting that *The Gospel of Mary Magdalene* was written in the fifth century CE, and even forget to mention that the later discoveries (the two copies in Greek) are dated to the third century CE. Scholars who work with the Gnostic Gospels, say that both the Coptic and Greek copies are just the surviving papyri of *The Gospel of Mary Magdalene* and that there must have been earlier versions. They estimate that *The Gospel of Mary Magdalene* is at least as old as 150 CE.

There is no doubt this dispute is much more than a scholarly disagreement, and academics make careers out of these kinds of arguments. It is also an ideological battle. *The Gospel of Mary Magdalene* not only describes more radical teachings of Jesus but also provides a disparaging view of the dynamic between the disciples; Peter is often represented as a resentful and angry disciple, and Mary Magdalene is shown as the receiver of the esoteric teachings of Jesus. Placing the dating of *The Gospel of Mary Magdalene* as later than the biblical gospels indirectly also disputes the special position of Mary Magdalene in Jesus' circles. On the other side of the coin, by dating it as closer to the biblical gospels, this reinforces the value of the esoteric teachings of *The Gospel of Mary Magdalene*.

Although it is important not to get lost in scholarly debates about which was first and which came after, a scholarly analysis needs to be encouraged. Each thorough investigation should check the facts that are known to us. At the same time, I would like to stress that what is known to us is the essential phrase here, because usually there are background stories and developments, both historical and more obscure, that may never be known to us. For the sake of our investigation, I would like to focus on the purpose of all sacred texts, which are always a message for humanity. The reason these texts were first passed on in oral form and then written down is to preserve their unique message for us.

Most sacred texts have ancient and often mysterious origins. It is claimed by many traditions that they were originally transmitted via energy for the sages who were able to receive this. For example, the ancient Hindu scriptures, the Vedas, were apparently transmitted via energy transfer, and others, like *The Gospel of Mary Magdalene*, were found in strange places and often under unusual circumstances.

How can things be passed on via energy? They can be what, in more modern renditions, are called downloads, or transferred telepathically. Such things not only happened in the past but continue to happen to the present day, and many people claim to have received a download, whether through a lucid dream, an anomalous encounter, in meditation, or otherwise. I personally believe that ancient texts were preserved for our benefit and were transmitted from the Source to the sages or sometimes to people who happened to be available and open-minded, and that this process did not necessarily stop in ancient times. It is more than likely that this transmission will continue, as we need it now more than ever.

Before I go in depth into the text itself, I would like to state that I am relying on the translation and interpretation of *The Gospel of Mary Magdalene* by a French scholar, therapist, former Catholic priest, and now an Eastern Orthodox priest, Jean-Yves Leloup that was published in English in 2002. I have chosen this translation and based my own interpretation on the groundwork Leloup has done because I sincerely believe he is not only a scholar but also a spiritual seeker. Unlike others, he has approached *The Gospel of Mary Magdalene* as if it is a sacred text that wants to teach us something. He has approached it with love, respect, and devotion. This is how the sacred texts want to be treated. These are not just old papyri or scrolls in some form to be dissected and studied. They are salient messengers from other realms and levels of consciousness with which we have only occasional access.

The messages are the pathways to the Divine, to the Source, and to our own self-realization and ascension, but only if we approach them in a loving and respectful way. This is what I wish for everyone who wants to study any esoteric or sacred text of any tradition: love it, give it your time, and listen to what it wants to tell you. Although I eventually came up with my own interpretation of *The Gospel of Mary Magdalene*, I acknowledge that, without the foundations set by Leloup, I would not have been able to do so.

Also, as a personal confession, I began to study *The Gospel of Mary Magdalene* in December 2004; I have spent a considerable amount of time with it and loved it for many decades. The circumstances of how I came across this text are described in my book *The Other Goddess*. Just before my trip to Jerusalem, a certain adventurer passed *The Gospel of Mary Magdalene* to me as a gift. I had no idea at the time that it would set me on a completely new path.

The simplest way of describing the content of *The Gospel of Mary Magdalene* is that it is divided into two parts. This division was probably not intentional and can be treated in two ways. The first reason for the division is an obvious, practical one, as several pages are missing. For example, what we have now starts on page 6, with pages 1 to 5 missing. Then, again in the middle of *The Gospel of Mary Magdalene*, pages 11 to 14 are missing. They are very important pages, as this is where the Jesus' crucifixion was most likely described. The second reason may be content related, as the *Gospel* is divided into teachings that Jesus gave with his own speech and teachings that only Mary Magdalene received from Jesus and afterwards shared with other disciples.

In the first part of *The Gospel of Mary Magdalene* (from pages 6 to 10), we see Jesus himself addressing questions from his male disciples. In part two (pages 15 to 19), we have Mary Magdalene addressing questions asked by the disciples. On page 9, line 5, Jesus' teachings end and we are told, "Having said all of this, he departed." On the same page, lines 6 to 11, the disciples' despair at the Teacher's departure, which we can assume is a reference to his death on the cross. They ask themselves how they can spread his teachings among the "unbelievers" when he has not been spared.

This is the exact moment when Mary Magdalene becomes prominent. She stands up and embraces the disciples as brothers. Mary Magdalene implores the male disciples not to despair but instead to allow his grace to guide them and comfort them. She advises them to speak of his greatness, for he had foreseen what would happen to him and what they would need to do after his departure. In short, she reminds them of their mission. This is a very interesting point for us to note: She does not tell them their mission is to teach unbelievers but rather to become *Anthropos*—Divine beings while in a human body. After this, all of them were uplifted and began pondering on her words.

On page 10, Peter and other disciples come to Mary Magdalene. Peter implores, "Sister, we know the Teacher loved you differently from other women. Tell us whatsoever you remember of any words he told you which we have not heard" (page 10, lines 1 to 6).

The division in content and the line above especially define the storyline of *The Gospel of Mary Magdalene*.

What is the plot of *The Gospel of Mary Magdalene*?

Keeping in mind that some pages are missing, we can see that the male disciples and Mary Magdalene gathered to ask questions of Jesus (part 1). The male disciple who asks questions of Jesus in part 1 is Peter. After answering Peter's questions, Jesus "departs." I believe it was assumed here readers would know what had happened to him. The disciples are distraught by his departure until Mary Magdalene stands up and reminds them of their mission. After this reminder, the disciples try to understand Jesus' teachings by asking Mary Magdalene to share with them what Jesus taught to her but not to them.

Mary Magdalene tells them how she encountered Jesus in a supernatural vision and shares the teachings that he conveyed to her in that space. The teachings she conveyed to the male disciples are what I believe are the teachings of ascension. At the end of her explanation, Andrew and Peter become angry that it was she—a woman—who had received the teachings they know nothing about. In their anger, they decide that Jesus could not possibly have said such things to her and not to them! At this point, Mary Magdalene begins to cry, asking Peter if he truly believes that she would lie about his teachings. Levy comes to her rescue and scolds Peter by reminding him that he (Peter) has always been hotheaded, and surely Peter knows that the Teacher "knew her very well, for he loved her more than us" (page 18, lines 13, 14).

Let's dive into the deep waters of the meaning of *The Gospel of Mary Magdalene.* In my opinion, Leloup, the translator and commentator of that sacred text, laid the best foundations for an explanation of the teachings of the *Gospel.* As a priest, he is aware of the teachings of the canonical Bible. As a spiritual seeker, he is also familiar with the esoteric traditions of Christianity, which were lost or rejected in the process of the compiling of the canonical Bible, sometime between the second and fourth centuries CE.

Moreover, as a scholar, Leloup knows the intellectual climate of the times in which both the canonical Bible and the esoteric sources were written. All of these things are important when deciphering a sacred text. The usual polarity in interpretations lies between the fundamentalist believers and scholars, as one group are convinced that what they are reading is a word-by-word passage told by God without any alterations, while the others look at the text within the intellectual climate of the times in which it was written.

This is my take on this debate. Even if someone chooses to believe a particular sacred text is the literal word of God, this does not mean the intellectual climate of the times in which the teachings were transferred is not important. I would like to give an example of a radio wave here. The same message will come through with different clarity depending on the station and the quality of connection. A much better example are the radio telescopes that astronomical observatories use to catch signals from space. Depending on the direction, power, advancement, and many other things, the signal will come through with different intensity or clarity. Even under the best of circumstances, a message might be scrambled and most likely incomplete.

The same is true of human receivers. We are not islands. We are people of our times, influenced positively or negatively by narratives that academics like to call "discourses." Everything we learn and everything that comes to us is filtered by those narratives, beliefs, prejudices, etc. The message might be pure, but the person receiving it might not even be aware of his or her conditioning, which is influenced by the times and even by geography. I believe these are the key things to remember when approaching a sacred text: the times and geography in which it was produced or transmitted and the actual teachings. Leloup considered these things carefully, and I have thrown a few extra ones into the mix.

Let's start with Leloup's interpretation. He wisely refers to the dominant philosophy when *The Gospel of Mary Magdalene* was compiled and which early Christian commentators, whether esoteric or biblical, drew from. They often relied on the teachings of the Greek philosopher Plato and philosophers belonging to the Neoplatonic school of thought. The Neoplatonists, as Leloup prefers to refer to them, set the matrix for an understanding of the Universe in their time in the same way as we today rely on hardcore science.

Nowadays, when we want to win an argument, we say, "Science says..." In the early centuries of the common area, people would say, "The Neoplatonists say…" Leloup draws heavily from both the Bible and Neoplatonism when explaining *The Gospel of Mary Magdalene*. This has helped him to notice one extremely important thing in the *Gospel* that everyone else has missed: the first four levels of consciousness. This is the fundamental teaching of *The Gospel of Mary Magdalene*. Leloup notes that before Mary Magdalene speaks of the last seven obstacles to the ascension of the soul, she gives considerable time to explaining the four levels through which a human soul needs to move to ascend. Only at the very end of her teachings does she explain the last seven obstacles. Unfortunately, modern interpretations, with the exception of Leloup, begin with the last seven elements.

Others, some of them very popular writers, immediately jump into the last seven obstacles to ascension, not realizing they have missed the basics! I think this is a modern thing—rushing to conclusions and offering solutions rather than patiently considering the main issue from the very beginning, which is the cause of the problem to start with. I made the same mistake when I started writing on this, but I have an opportunity here to correct it.

When Mary Magdalene gives the teachings of the ascension of the soul, she describes the first four levels through which the soul must pass before it reaches liberation.

What are the first four levels? In the text they are:

Level 1 – (pages missing)

Level 2 – Wrong desire

Level 3 – Ignorance (limiting knowledge)

Level 4 – The wrath of the last seven elements, which are what Leloup calls the "last violent feelings" and what I call the "last remains of negative tendencies."

How do we know what the first level is? We know because *The Gospel of Mary Magdalene* conveys the same message that the Neoplatonists and also other esoteric traditions propose: Level 1 is wrong identification.

Therefore, the four levels needed for the soul to overcome so it can ascend are: wrong identification, wrong desire, ignorance, and the wrath of the last seven elements—the "last violent feelings" or last remains of negative tendencies.

Leloup points out that each of the four levels has two movements or two "climates" which can move the soul either higher (ascent) or lower (descent) from its current state. He overlaps the four levels with Neoplatonic terminology and consequently assigns the term *soma* to the first level; *psyche* to the second level; *nous* to the third level; and *pneuma* to the fourth level. The esoteric terminology is, at times, complex, but we reap rewards of initiation if we make the effort to explain them, and this is what the next part of this chapter will do.

Now let's move to how it is explained in *The Gospel of Mary Magdalene* and what this means in practice, in my interpretation and experience. I am deeply grateful for Leloup's soulful translation and meticulous spiritual interpretation, but I think we can take it further.

What happens at the first level when we experience identification?

This is our identification with the material world only. At this stage of consciousness, we are only concerned with "getting ahead," having a career, a family, a nice car, and a nice house. There is nothing wrong with any of these things, as long as we do not assume that there is nothing else. And this is the main point of the first level. At this level, we assume that there is nothing else. Moreover, we are willing to argue scientifically that there is nothing beyond matter and we rely solely on hardcore materialistic science, which tells us we were at first animal-like and then, out of the blue, we developed some awareness. At this level, we believe that we are nothing else but bodies with a bigger brain and we should use our intelligence to get to the top of the food chain. Ideally, we might also get rich and famous as we are doing this.

We ridicule other people who think differently, even members of our own family or good friends. We call them naive, misguided, eccentric, or "out there." At very best, we might call them a sensitive soul or an artistic soul. At this stage of consciousness development, we believe that we are always right, and we quietly ridicule people who have otherworldly experiences, whether spiritual, anomalous, parapsychological, etc. Most importantly, we are completely focused on the external world because we are believers that all that is important lies outside of ourselves and we need to do our best to get or achieve this. In this state of consciousness, we are convinced that all things good and bad come from the outside. Our success, or lack of it, is explained either through good luck, connections, external efforts, or "being in the know" and "knowing the tricks of the trade" well.

An excellent quote from *The Gospel of Mary Magdalene* pertaining to the first level comes from Jesus on page 8 where he warns us to be vigilant and not to allow anyone to deceive us by telling us that external things would lead us to fulfillment. What we seek, the Teacher says, is within us.

I think this is a very poignant passage, especially in our times, when so many things are built to distract us from the greatness that lives within us. Whether it is social media, news, or a specific YouTube channel, or the need to know all world events, the diversion from our inner world is there. I am not even including our constant preoccupation with survival. In my darker moods, I agree with some Gnostic schools that our three-dimensional reality is set up this way, so we live in constant fear for our and our family's survival.

What is the upside of this setup? Our fear might propel us to work on ourselves, on our own spirituality, to move to a higher level of ascended consciousness.

Once, at a conference, I was asked how one can move from the first to the second level. This is a very valid question and I could only answer with examples that others had shared with me: it could be a life changing or even a life threatening event; an invitation to a retreat that we have suddenly decided to follow up on, even if it is completely out of our ordinary modus operandi; or, as in one case, a book fell off the shelf onto someone and the unusual event encouraged the person to read the book and that, in turn, changed them. Alternatively, sometimes people talk of encountering the title of some film, book, or the name of the place that prompts them to respond to these synchronicities.

What happens on the second level, when we experience the wrong desire?

At the second level, we are slightly more conscious, as we are at least aware of our own drives and desires and we know that they come from within. In fact, the Platonic concept of the *psyche* is often understood as the life force that guides us. The *psyche* comes from and is connected to the World of Ideas, which is a higher reality good matrix, so to speak, from which all things derive. In this interpretation, the *psyche* is a reminder of our soul and purpose and the desires she stores in our memories from a higher dimension. This can help to remind us of our higher purpose and belonging. Here we are not solely victims of external demands and stimuli, as we were at the first level.

Many of us can identify with this second level of consciousness as the *psyche*. Indeed, many of us have dreams of fulfilment through a particular profession, calling, or societal role, such as "I am a mother or a father." Ambition falls into this category as well. There are two ways in which we can deal with our desires: We can either surrender to the lowest point and become victims of our own drives, or we can direct them to the highest point and, in this way, fulfill our highest potential as well.

What are the quotes from *The Gospel of Mary Magdalene* that testify to this interpretation of the second level?

On page 7, Peter asks Jesus to define the "sin of the world." Jesus answers that "there is no sin." Then he continues to explain that it is we who make sin's existence possible by acting according to the inclination of our "corrupted nature," which I would call lower levels of consciousness. What we need to do to avoid habitual bad choices is to reunite ourselves with our higher nature.

This is one of my favorite quotes in *The Gospel of Mary Magdalene*, and I am aware that this is the very same quote that will trigger some people who read it superficially. Jesus says that sin is redeemable; that is, it is a consequence of bad habits. As mentioned before, at the second level, we have a choice to act from our lower or higher nature. It may take more effort to act from our higher nature, but this action alone brings us back to our Divine origins. Every single moment of our lives, we have a choice to act from our selfish, ego-centered nature, which considers what is good only for us, or to act from our selfless nature, which brings good to everyone. My advice is, if you do not know what to do in a given situation and are tempted to act selfishly, just do the opposite! Or do what a Great Being aligned with his or her Divine purpose would do.

What is a practical example of this?

When I was a very young woman and student of theoretical philosophy at the Catholic University in Lublin, Poland, I attended a lecture by Victor Frankl. I did not know anything about him then and was told that he was a famous philosopher and psychologist. He was already very old and frail, but his talk changed my life. I did not know then that he was also a Holocaust survivor from Auschwitz, as I knew nothing of his past or life. I only knew he was famous.

He told us two things that I will always remember. One of them was a sweet personal story. He was born in Austria and as young boy he dreamed about being a famous psychoanalyst like Sigmund Freud. One day, while walking in a park in Vienna, the young Viktor came across Freud. Overjoyed by his incredible luck, he engaged him in a conversation. Freud and Frankl sat on a park bench and Freud answered all the questions that the young Frankl had for him. It was a significant conversation because, in his eighties,

Frankl still remembered it as a turning point in his life. At this moment, Frankl chose his life path: He wanted to be just like Sigmund Freud.

This was the first part of his story, leading to the second and the most important part which, in turn, changed my life. Frankl told us that, when young and very accomplished in his field, he still suffered from a very strong desire to become as famous as Freud or Carl Jung. Because of this, none of his own accomplishments could satisfy him. I could relate to his desire because I, too, had an overpowering desire to become a famous writer.

The auditorium was full. There must have been hundreds of people there, but I felt like it was just Frankl and me. It felt personal. I wanted to know how he fulfilled his desire for fame.

I noticed that suddenly, his demeanor changed from serious to amused, as if he knew someone really, really needed to hear what he had to say. And this what he told us: "One day, I gave up. I tried so hard to be at my best and write books, but fame evaded me. So, I told myself, 'It looks like I will never become famous anyway, so I will stop writing books that I think will make me famous and I will write a book that will help others.'"

He smiled when he said, "And that was the book that made me famous."

I remember standing there in the huge auditorium, among hundreds of students, thinking, "I need to remember this! This is something I need to know."

This is how Frankl redirected his desire from selfishness to selflessness and received what he wanted. He did not stop writing. He did not give up doing what he had always done so well and become a car salesman. Instead, he simply did what he had always done, but with a higher intention.

And this is exactly what can happen at the second level of the ascension of consciousness—choosing action from a higher perspective. The opposite to this is something that we observe all too often, when we see ourselves or others losing integrity to achieve a goal. It might be an actor sleeping with a film director to get a part or a businessperson signing a profitable deal at the expense of the natural environment. It might be a politician who makes promises but is only interested in gaining power over others. These are choices. One leads to ascension, while the other takes us back to the first level.

What happens at the third level when we experience the conflict between the wrong knowledge and wisdom? What is the role of *nous* there?

When we pass through the challenges of the first level of being, caught entirely in the limitations of the materialistic point of view, and we manage to transform our desire by pointing it towards a higher good on the second level, we face the third challenge in the process of ascension: overcoming ignorance and opening to deeper insight. Like everything during the process of ascension outlined in *The Gospel of Mary Magdalene*, the third level has two possible outcomes: lower and higher. The lower outcome keeps us in the throes of limiting knowledge, which is a form of ignorance.

What is ignorance? It is limiting ourselves to what we already know and refusing to open our minds to higher wisdom. I would even go as far as to say that it is limiting ourselves to only understanding the material and refusing spiritual insight or any perception or understanding that challenges our current view of reality. In many ways, the third level is closely connected to the first level. At the first level, we are bound to materialistic reality, but at the third level we are bound to a perception of material reality. The third level can also be seen as a refusal to open up to other forms of perception beyond what is possible in the physical realm.

The higher end of the third level is the opposite. We open our field of perception beyond the physical and we are open to spiritual, multidimensional, or simply unusual insights and experiences. I put insight and experience in one sentence, one after another, because it can be exceedingly difficult to experience spiritual or multidimensional realities without being open to the possibility of such perception or experience.

In *The Gospel of Mary Magdalene*, at the third level of ascension, we are introduced to the concept of *nous*. *Nous* is a hook that connects our soul with Source or Eternity or Divine Wisdom. It is the very tip of our soul, after which there is only *pneuma* or pure spirit. For those who struggle with this kind of terminology, *nous* is the finest point of perception available to us. In other words, it is our ability to perceive the immaterial, spiritual, or interdimensional—while we are still in our human body.

For me, one of the most poignant moments of *The Gospel of Mary Magdalene* occurs when the male disciples ask her to share with them the teachings that Jesus has shared only with her. The answer she gives them is not what one would expect, and it will be a specific challenge for those who have issues with the possibility of *nous* in human experience.

On page 10, Mary Magdalene reveals that she had a vision of the Teacher and said to him, "Lord, I see you in this vision." And Jesus answered, "You are blessed, for the sight of me does not disturb you." There, where the *nous* is, lies the treasure.

This is significant because Mary Magdalene is told she is "blessed" because she can see him when others can't. She is open to the perception of the spiritual, while others expect to see him in body. Moreover, she is told that having access to *nous* is a treasure, a gift—to be open to this more subtle field of perception. Mary Magdalene is curious about the status of *nous* in the spiritual world or even between levels of ascension, so she asks Jesus if *nous* is like the soul (*psyche)* or like pure spirit (*pneuma*). Jesus explains that it is neither, as *nous* lies in between the *psyche* and *pneuma* and therefore between the second and fourth level.

Let's pause for a moment and absorb this instruction, as it teaches us that it is in the liminal space, the in-between, where the miraculous and unusual happen.

I find this interesting because I believe it might also explain why some people have spiritual experiences and some don't, or why some people have other anomalous experiences and others in their presence don't. As far as anomalous or interdimensional experiences are concerned, there are many instances of these. For example, in the town of Fatima, Portugal in 1917, most people there experienced *something* spiritual, or at least anomalous, but there was a group of people there at the same time who did not see or experience anything at all.

Whether we speak of spiritual perceptions and experiences or other anomalous experiences is a matter of interpretation. Often, spiritual people believe that they have experienced something deeply spiritual, while, for example, UFO researchers believe that they have seen a spaceship. Either way, both have experienced what they did because of their ability to perceive beyond the material. *Nous* is the tool and it is available to us, within us. I would like to suggest that all our "supernatural" experiences are related to this ability and only our interpretations of the experiences differ, as in the case of the Fatima sightings-visitations.

What are practical examples of the lower end of the third level—that is, the other side of the coin where *nous* is not acknowledged?

This might be a scientist who releases an invention even if it harms the planet or humanity. Personally, I would put in this category many AI scientists and companies that appear to act without respect for biological life or spirituality. These kinds of scientists do not understand the depth of consciousness and its connection with Source. They confuse information and speed of calculation and processing of information with consciousness. They are like mathematically brilliant children who create without consideration for the consequences of their actions. They create either from the first level (a full identification with material existence), the second level (wrong desire), or the third level (ignorance or lack of awareness of higher levels of perception). I will return to this point later when giving examples of the fourth level.

A more immediate example, which is so prevalent in most media at the moment, is the ridiculing of people who share their spiritual or anomalous experiences. Our own lack of this kind of experience does not invalidate someone else's experience. I understand that this might be stretching our convictions at times, and it does not mean we should abandon all discernment—but we should be open-minded. I also have limits to what is acceptable for me in the area of the anomalous experience and often use my analytical mind to consider these phenomena as well. But I have stopped discrediting them simply because they are, at least initially, confronting to my mind.

What happens on the fourth level when we experience the last assault of wrong tendencies?

At the fourth level, we deal with the wrath of the last seven elements, which are what Leloup calls the "last violent feelings" and which I call the last remains of negative tendencies. My spiritual teacher from another esoteric tradition called these "tearing thoughts"—the lower creations of our own mind that resist change and transformation.

At this level, we are asked to give up our small self to be able to embody our highest Self. *Pneuma* is the Pure Spirit, the highest level of human spiritual development. This is when we become Anthropos, according to *The Gospel of Mary Magdalene*. Leloup equates this with the Holy Spirit which corresponds well, he claims, with the philosophical systems of Platonism and Neoplatonism, as well as with the Hebrew tradition of *Ruah* or the Divine Breath. I would like to add that in esoteric Gnostic and Hindu traditions, this refers to either *Sophia* which is understood as Holy Wisdom or *Shakti-Kundalini*, coined as Life Force—both of which are feminine aspects of the Spirit. I refer to this as "Goddess Consciousness."

For people who have issues with my terminology, there are more neutral names for *pneuma*, such as Cosmic Consciousness, Christ Consciousness, or Unifying Consciousness. Leloup likes to call it the "Holy Spirit" or "Grace." At this level of consciousness, after we let go of the last remnants of lower energies within our being, the Pure Spirit descends upon us. We now live in a state of Grace. This is what other traditions refer to as "Enlightenment."

In other words, our ascension activates the movement of Pure Spirit towards us, which is beautifully elucidated by a favorite line in *The Gospel of Mary Magdalene,* so masterfully translated by Leloup:

I left the world with the aid of another world;
a design was erased,
by virtue of a higher design[16].

This wonderful quote has two meanings: Not only does the Pure Spirit descend on us and pull us up, but our individual ascension also triggers a collective ascension. What does this mean? This means that if we, individually, try to ascend, the whole of our reality ascends with us. Not only are we transformed, but the whole universe transforms and is taken to a higher level of spiritual evolution. We are that powerful.

What are the final obstacles of wrath mentioned in *The Gospel of Mary Magdalene?*

They are the seven manifestations of wrath as the last remnants of lower energies within us, which could include any or all of Darkness, Craving, Ignorance, Lethal Jealousy, Enslavement to the Body, Intoxicated Knowledge, and Guileful Knowledge. The last two are forms of knowledge based on the desires of the ego rather than on deeper wisdom. They oppress the soul with questions such as: "Where do you come from, murderer?" and "Where are you going, vagabond?"[17]

These are questions with which the dying lower energies torment the ascending soul. They are questions of self-doubt that turn our minds against us. In fact, it is not that the ascending soul is dying, it is that the lower energies within us are dying. They attempt to send their Wrath at us as a last, pathetic attempt to bring us down to their mercy again. It is of highest importance not to give in to these voices. If we do, we fall one level at a time, until we are back at the first level again.

An example of this mind-attack would be an individual who chooses to take the road less traveled, to speak metaphorically. Instead of following the crowd, they turn to their own inner voice and refine it until they can trust that it truly is their inner voice and not that of lower energies attempting to pull them down.

As an example, let's say you have made a conscious decision to make a higher choice: you have graduated with a veterinary degree and signed up to help in a wildlife sanctuary. This choice gives you immense satisfaction and you feel you are connected to something higher than yourself through your service. But now and then, you are assaulted by lower energies that tell you that you are a loser.

"Who do you think you are?" they ask you, "to think you can make a difference?"

Alternatively, the opposite is also true: it is not about what we choose, but whether our choice is aligned with our highest version of ourselves. For example, for my PhD, I interviewed a successful musician who had been told by his father to study veterinary science. Instead, he had chosen to play the piano for twelve hours every day, as doing so connected him to his true self. However, years later, he told me that he knew—yes *knew,* with that higher knowing—that it was his calling to write an opera about the brutal beginnings of Australia.

I asked him at the time, "Why don't you do this?" and he answered that it was "not that simple." He was now used to receiving awards each year for his film scores, and working on that opera would put him "out of sight" for a long time. I like this example because it shows that the same person can make higher or lower choices, and therefore ascend or descend, multiple times at different periods of their lives.

These are the practical tools that are offered in *The Gospel of Mary Magdalene*. However, few choose to notice them. These are the very same tools that uplift our consciousness and sharpen our sense of perception. Then, and only then, we can fully distinguish the different versions of reality that we are presented with. I believe that the tools relate to the choices given to us by the beings visiting us: one takes us to spiritual evolution, the other towards merging with technology. The choice is always our own—one path leads to the ascent and the other to the descent of our consciousness.

THE GOSPEL OF MARY MAGDALENE AND THE EGYPTIAN ESOTERIC TRADITIONS

We need to understand the difficulties in deciphering the esoteric teachings of *The Gospel of Mary Magdalene* because, as for many of these sorts of texts, it was written in such a way that would make sense to initiates but not to outsiders. This is why it is useful to refer to other esoteric traditions with which the transmitters of *The Gospel of Mary Magdalene* were in contact. They lived with these ideas and their intellectual and geographical influences.

I think that too often, this Gospel is read only within the Judeo-Christian tradition—I include Leloup's reading in this—with rare escapades to the world view at the time it was written. People seem to forget one extremely important thing: *The Gospel of Mary Magdalene* was found, and mostly likely also written, in Egypt. For this reason alone, we need to consider the esoteric traditions of Egypt at that time.

The Egyptian tradition that I would like to focus on is the myth of the Goddess Isis and Osiris, but before we can do this, we need to look into the historical evidence of this myth. Let's start with the mundane version of the story of Isis as has been conveyed to us by mainstream Egyptologists and the

Encyclopedia Britannica. According to mainstream scholarship, Isis was first heard of around 2500 BCE, and in this first reference, she is not really known as a goddess but rather as a queen to the Pharaoh Osiris. This, in itself, is a juicy moment in our detective journey, as we have already started to suspect that all other goddesses appeared in human bodies as well, including Inanna and Demeter.

Isis and Osiris ruled happily over Egypt until Osiris' brother Seth became jealous and set out to kill him. Seth's killing of Osiris gives us the first known story of a king being killed, put in a wooden chest, and left to float on the Nile. Isis, who was missing her husband, searched for him until she found some of his remains in the chest. The story is not very clear at this point. Some of the remains were missing, because the evil Seth had cut Osiris' body into pieces and spread them around Egypt. With the help of her sister, Nephthys, Isis transformed herself into a bird and flew far and wide searching for the rest of her husband's body. She did not stop until she put together all the pieces of her husband's body—except his penis.

And here, for the first time, we hear about Isis' magical powers: Through using her magic, she reassembled him. We can assume that she also magically created his penis and attached it to the rest of his body. Some versions state that she found it in the current location of the Temple of Isis on the island of Philae. Presumably, they then made love, because soon after, she gave a birth to their child, Horus, who eventually avenged his father by killing Seth.

This version of the story of Isis, Osiris, and Horus reminds me a little of mainstream religions and mainstream media; it only tells a part of the story and focuses on the plot instead of the meaning. This version does not want us to understand anything that will actually help us to learn from the myth and evolve. To understand the esoteric version of the story, we need to turn to Paul Brunton and his book, *A Search in Secret Egypt.*

Initially, I came across Brunton's work while I was a part of a community diligently studying Hindu esoteric teachings. I'd had spiritual experiences related to this tradition and I was looking for someone who had been on the same spiritual search, had had similar experiences, and could give me some explanations. My spiritual teacher at the time suggested I read Brunton's *A Search in Secret India*, which I did when participating in a spiritual retreat in 2010.

A Search in Secret India, first published in 1934, became an instant bestseller and was republished dozens of times. The edition I was working with was published in 2003. Brunton's book describes his own experiences, including meeting some of India's greatest spiritual teachers. The book influenced me profoundly and confirmed some of my own spiritual experiences. So, when I began my studies of *The Gospel of Mary Magdalene*, I was delighted to learn that a few years after writing about his experiences in India, in 1936, Paul Brunton published *A Search in Secret Egypt* about his experiences in Egypt.

I think it is important to state that I consider Brunton a sincere spiritual seeker and teacher, one of the few people who made the effort not only to acquire esoteric knowledge—which is difficult enough—but also to travel to the places where the teachings originated. The book describes his own experiences while on that search. Also, when he came back from his journeys, he spent the rest of his days living a quiet life in Switzerland, writing more books on spirituality and rejecting any offer of being engaged or popularized as a spiritual teacher. He did not seek fame. In fact, he avoided it, preferring to put his experiences and ideas on paper for other seekers like himself.

A Search in Secret Egypt follows the same format structurally as *A Search in Secret India*. After describing meeting a few magicians and tricksters who have managed to gain some access to the anomalous, he eventually shares his own experiences, including those with eternal beings who, according to him, still live in Egypt and are available to true seekers. One of the most striking experiences Brunton describes is when he is inside the Great Pyramid of Giza. Thanks to important dignitaries pulling some strings, he is allowed to spend a night alone inside the Great Pyramid. He is given an armed guard who waits for him outside at the exit and is available in case he encounters any danger. The rest is an exceptional story.

After a detailed description of all of the Great Pyramid's chambers, Brunton uses a meditation technique he had learned in India. He sits in complete darkness in one of the chambers. There, he is faced with malevolent spirits who try to frighten him and convince him to abandon his experiment. Through his learning in India, Brunton is able to continue witnessing the "sinister" and "hellish" beings without allowing them to force him out of the pyramid. Since he is unmoved by their attempts, they suddenly disappear.

Then Brunton becomes conscious of another, benevolent presence who asks him, "Why are you here?" and warns him that "The Way of the Dream" may drive him mad. When the being cannot change Brunton's resolve, it agrees to take him to the "Hall of Learning." But Brunton first has to go to the King's Chamber and lie down inside the sarcophagus located there.

Once in the sarcophagus, Brunton begins feeling heavy and numb. An "ice cold energy" moves through his body. He seems to "whirl" and "pass upward through a narrow hole" to a place where he feels completely free. This must have been an out-of-body experience, as he recounts that he was lifted horizontally with his feet first until he steadies himself to be in an upward position. He can see his body still lying in the sarcophagus. Emotionally, Brunton describes feeling that he was leaving everything behind, including everything and everyone he knows. He even left the people whom he had once loved and were now deceased.

The being that guided him, whom he began referring to as the priest, prays to the Egyptian God Amun "to turn his face upon his son." At this stage, Brunton receives teachings that instruct him to find the passage in his mind to the Divine Mind. After this, Brunton finds himself back inside the sarcophagus in the King's Chamber.

Brunton's writing about his experience encouraged some other brave souls to also spend a night in the Great Pyramid of Giza. When I was interviewed on a podcast discussing Egyptian mysteries, the interviewer told me that, many years before, after reading Brunton's book, he had endeavored to do the same. Through his personal connections in Egypt, he was allowed to spend the night in the Great Pyramid. He, too, was assaulted by some malevolent elemental beings, just as Brunton had been at the beginning. The energy that the interviewer felt from them was so intrusive and malignant that it was all he could do to retain his energy intact through conscious breathing and to eventually leave the pyramid. The interviewer did not come across as someone easily frightened; however, in his experience, he believed it was not safe to stay inside the pyramid.

Brunton was also the first person who, through his books, explained the esoteric interpretation of the myth of Isis, Osiris, and their child Horus in a way that made sense to me. According to Brunton, there is more to this resurrection story than we have been told. In his understanding, Isis represents the *hierophant*, the guide, the necessary element, as it is she who performs the ritual of resurrection or who teaches us that there is life after death. Osiris represents humans, or more precisely initiates, who are ready to absorb this knowledge while still alive. This happens through the ritual, which takes them temporarily out of their bodies to see the spiritual or other dimensional world.

Horus, the child conceived by Isis when, through magic, she manages to temporarily revive Osiris, represents awakened humanity. On a more individual level, Horus represents an awakened initiate who has undergone the ritual and now knows the truth about our reality and other realities. As in the case of the Eleusinian Mysteries, the initiates were sworn to complete secrecy.

Overall, the myth of Isis and Osiris represents a ritual through which chosen initiates were taken to a sacred place to undergo secret rites. The ritual was designed to prove to them that there was a spiritual realm after we leave the body, either through death or through the sacred and secret ritual and an out-of-body experience, as Brunton was shown in the Great Pyramid of Giza.

Later in the book, Brunton finds evidence of the ritual in the temples of Karnak which he calls "the headquarters of the Egyptian priesthood." He describes in detail four panels showing the Pharoah Rameses IV in four stages of initiation by the Goddess Amunet. The Goddess points to an *ankh* between the Pharaoh's eyes. In Ancient Egypt, an *ankh* was a sacred symbol. It is a combination of a cross, representing the death-like mysteries, and a serpent-like circle symbolizing eternity, or no beginning and no end. The space between the eyes is where the pineal gland is situated and is a center of attention and spiritual awakening in nearly all esoteric traditions I have studied.

The panels in Karnak depict upright cobras (symbolizing awakening) moving towards the Pharoah, who is about to be initiated by the Goddess. Here the Pharoah is the initiate (like Osiris), the Goddess Amunet is the hierophant-deity (like Isis), and Horus is the awakened initiate with his fingers upon his lips, symbolizing the secret aspect of the ritual. As with the Eleusinian Mysteries, anyone who was of any standing in society at that time sought to be initiated.

Originally, only the high initiates were allowed to participate, but later the pharaohs sought initiation as well. We also know that the Greek philosophers Thales, Pythagoras, and Plato did so, as did Solon, a statesman and philosopher who is counted among the Seven Great Sages of Ancient Greece.

Let's move along on our detective journey and consider how the Ancient Egyptian tradition of initiation in ascension to higher levels—an initiation in which Isis or Hathor or Amunet played a crucial role—might affect the ascension levels in *The Gospel of Mary Magdalene.*

I find the similarity astounding between the four levels of consciousness in *The Gospel of Mary Magdalene* and the four panels in the temples of Karnak showing the Ancient Egyptian ritual of initiation. In both the Ancient Egyptian ritual and the *Gospel,* the feminine presence plays an important part, as a teacher, hierophant, or guide, or as a final vision. In Brunton's case, at the end of his book, the final vision he receives is that of the Goddess Isis.

Another similarity between the Ancient Egyptian rituals, which were held only for initiates and pharaohs, and Gnostic texts such as *The Gospel of Mary Magdalene* is the three-layered meaning of the teachings. When I began to study Gnostic Christian texts—the texts that present a more esoteric teaching aspect of Jesus' teachings—I learned that, according to many Gnostic schools, Jesus gave three levels of teachings. The first and most basic one was for the fishermen and farmers around the lake of Galilee, where he often taught. The second level was for his closer followers such as his disciples, later called the Apostles. And the third level of teaching was those he gave to his most advanced disciples, amongst whom was Mary Magdalene.

The plot of *The Gospel of Mary Magdalene* clearly shows other disciples coming to her for guidance after the Teacher is crucified, as he had shared more advanced wisdom with her and not with them. This is also what, in the end, upset Peter and Andrew, once they realized that they had no clue what she had been talking about. They resented that the Teacher had found her more worthy of these teachings.

In *A Search in Secret Egypt*, Brunton explains that the Ancient Egyptian hieroglyphics had three levels of meaning as well. The first level of meaning was very basic and literal, so anyone who could read hieroglyphics would understand them at the face value. For example, an ibis is a type of bird, and a cow is a type of animal. The second level of meaning was for the priesthood, who could understand the more advanced meanings behind the symbols, such as the ibis represents Thoth, and the cow represents the Goddess Hathor or the Goddess Isis. Only the initiated would understand the much deeper meaning of the symbols, that the ibis represents a higher level of consciousness or ascension and the cow represents the role of Isis in the ritual of initiation.

Let's now apply the esoteric symbolism of Ancient Egypt to *The Gospel of Mary Magdalene* and see whether they correspond to each other. The first level noted in the *Gospel* refers to the three-dimensional consciousness that acknowledges and understands only the physical and the material. Classically, in most esoteric traditions, we cannot progress from this level unless through some inner impulse or, more often, when some external event shocks us and, as a result, we begin looking for answers, as our old understanding of the world does not make sense anymore. This is what happened to Osiris when he was killed by his evil brother, Seth.

At the second level of *The Gospel of Mary Magdalene*, we begin to have a more complex understanding of our life and reality around us. This is represented by desire, which can either bring us down or uplift us and direct us to a higher purpose. This is when awakening begins and we become more open-minded. In Ancient Egyptian esoterica, it is represented by *djed*. At the most basic level of meaning, *djed* is a depiction of Osiris' spine. At the esoteric level, *djed* is a representation of the movement of ascension. Interestingly, the Hindu tradition also contains this idea, called *sushumna*, where all our desires are stored. In the Neoplatonist traditions, this is the *psyche*. At this level, we are still not aware of the eternal, but we have an inkling of understanding that perhaps not everything is mortal.

As we progress along our spiritual journey, we move on to the third level, which is particularly emphasized in *The Gospel of Mary Magdalene* as *nous*. *Nous* is the hook of our soul to eternity. It is where Mary Magdalene meets Jesus after his crucifixion and it is, in my understanding, also the mental space where all events and experiences that are now classified as anomalous are perceived and encountered. I would even suggest that, in our modern vocabulary, this is the space of interdimensionality, where I believe most anomalous encounters happen.

But first, we need to go within and turn away from external distractions. In Ancient Egyptian esoterica, this process of going within is represented by a *sekhem, which* is directly involved in helping us to ascend to higher levels of consciousness. It is a significant element of ascension that provides us with powerful insight—such as when Mary Magdalene saw Jesus after the Resurrection—and can also give us power. A *sekhem*, from which the English term the scepter is derived, has two ends: the bottom end gives us the power to rule over others while the upper end gives the power to evolve or to ascend. It is compelling to note that all monarchs and the Pope have a scepter and use it to have power over others. Therefore, *sekhem* represents both: our ability to perceive the anomalous including UFOs and the desire of some to suppress this information for their own ends.

The final level of ascension in *The Gospel of Mary Magdalene* is mostly concerned with getting rid of the last vestiges of the voice of the ego, either in the form "I am not worthy" or in the form "I am better than others." At this level, we get help from above. Divine wisdom reaches out to us to propel us higher on our ascension journey. In Ancient Egyptian esoterica, this level is represented by an *ankh*. An *ankh* usually accompanies Isis, who holds it as her insignia and the symbol of the peak of ascension. This is also where the higher magic of Isis happens. This is not some crude spell to obtain something, the way lower magic is used in basic witchery. Instead, this magic can affect the whole matrix of our reality. We can correct, at the highest level of Creation, what needs correcting because it has been corrupted. This is why I believe that spiritual ascension is the best kind of activism. It is a profound change within, at both the individual and collective levels. This is what esoteric texts teach us.

THE GOSPEL OF MARY MAGDALENE AND CARL JUNG

The esoteric texts that we are investigating here have a timeless value. I would argue that if we are willing to go through the processes they discuss and decipher the stories that they tell us, they can help us to understand the workings of our inner world and therefore assist us in the process of transformation. Yet, after the esoteric texts were found, translated, read, and interpreted, they were often treated as curiosities for the mystically minded and not necessarily helpful for a modern person.

I vehemently disagree with this opinion. So, when I was studying *The Gospel of Mary Magdalene* and its Egyptian predecessors, I kept asking myself how I could bring it to more modern scholarship and make it more available to the modern mind. When we ask ourselves this kind of question, the answer often comes in synchronistic ways. For more than a decade, as I was giving talks for Carl Jung Societies around Australia, I discovered that Jung had similar intuitions and interests.

Carl Jung was a Swiss psychoanalyst (1875-1961) who, until 1912, was known as the most gifted student of the famous psychoanalyst Sigmund Freud. In 1912, Jung had a fallout with his mentor over interpretations on the human psyche. Jung was also unsatisfied with the lack of spiritual outlook in Freud's theories.

In my desire to bring esoteric teachings, especially *The Gospel of Mary Magdalene*, more available to modern audiences, I discovered that Jung also had a fascination with the Gnostic teachings. He had made a connection between the story of Jesus' resurrection and the myth of Isis and Osiris and had many anomalous experiences that he describes in his autobiography, *Memories, Dreams and Recollections* (first published in English in 1961 as a translation from the German).

Jung signed one of his most esoteric works, *Seven Sermons to the Dead* (1916), as Basilides, who was a Gnostic from the early second century Alexandria, Egypt. Indeed, Jung's interest in esoterica, and the Gnostic teachings especially, was well known to those around him. When several Gnostic documents were found in 1945 in Nag Hammadi in Egypt, Jung's friends smuggled some of them from Egypt and gave them to Jung as a gift on his 80th birthday. This selection of documents is now known as the "Jung Codex." But this is just a side road on our detective journey, and I am sharing this because it is good to know that we have allies on our search.

In the process of going deeper into *The Gospel of Mary Magdalene* and its teachings on ascension—and the importance of *nous*—for our investigation, I realized that Jung's model of what he called "individuation" was parallel to the teachings of the *Gospel*, despite the fact that he did not know about its existence when he formulated his model. We are getting here to some heavy psychological terminology, so I will be brief but as thorough as possible.

It is essential for us to know that Jung defined individuation in *Two Essays on Analytical Psychology* (1992). According to Jung, individuation is "the process by which we bring together all our parts which results in creating and embracing the incompatible uniqueness of our individual self which I believe was always of a spiritual nature and the final point in the development of the human psyche."[18] He later added that this is, in fact, the process of self-realization.

I admit this is an academic mouthful, so let's quickly unpack it. In a few words, what does Jung mean here?

Jung means that to evolve spiritually and reach the peak of our existence, we need to work on ourselves. This includes embracing some parts of ourselves that we have banished because they are not accepted by our society, family, environment, etc. Now, embracing this takes exactly four stages to accomplish—just as in *The Gospel of Mary Magdalene*.

What are these stages? In Jungian terms, they are *persona*, *shadow*, *anima*, and *individuation* or the "fully realized self."

The *persona* is exactly that—our social persona, the identity that we create to be successful in life and accepted by society. This is our professional identity, or more broadly, our social identity. For example, we can identify as a professional person such as a professor, doctor, etc. or as a mother, father, or something else that we identify with that gives us both a sense of belonging and recognition. In principle, there is nothing wrong with the persona, except that this is not who we fully are. It is what Jung describes as only a "sliver of who we are."

This is our false or partial identity, which corresponds to the first level in *The Gospel of Mary Magdalene*. For example, my *persona* is my professional image. People often see me as an academic. This is my social mask that not only provides financially for me but is also something that people find worthy of respect. When I tell people I am an author, they ask, "Yeah, but what do you *really* do?" This used to drive me crazy but now I have learned that they are simply asking me, "What is your persona, Joanna?" They do not ask me, "Who are you?" or "How do you see yourself?" They ask me about my social role. In my social role as an academic, I am constricted and too afraid of being shamed, to cover topics such as UFOs, their relationship to AI and humanity in general. My persona knows that these topics are unacceptable in my current professional setting and even damaging to my career.

The second stage is the acknowledgment of our *shadow*. Our shadow is everything about ourselves that we reject for the sake of acceptance and success. In Jung's model, however, there is no way to advance without uncovering our shadow and incorporating it into our psyche and life. Indeed, the shadow is the key to the fulfilled self. Also, if we continue rejecting this part of ourselves, it will continue to sabotage us. Why? Because our shadow wants to be acknowledged.

In my experience, the shadow is often where our gifts lie—the very gifts that we are afraid to show to the world because we are afraid of being rejected, judged, or losing a job. For me, writing on topics seldom discussed in academic circles was exactly that. It allows me to show the other Joanna that is not seen by many people, and which could not be shown professionally.

In *The Gospel of Mary Magdalene*, the shadow is the desire that can either sabotage us or can take us further, depending on our choices.

The third stage is *anima*, which has a double meaning according to Jung: either as a soul or, more commonly, the female part of our psyche, which operates together with the *animus* which is the male part of our psyche. Both exist in different ratios in both sexes. How do we integrate the anima or animus? I think that we all know whether we operate mostly from the feminine or masculine side. For example, as an academic, I operated solely from my masculine side, as this is what was required to succeed. However, my feminine shadow was sabotaging me, because I was not integrating it into my life—or at least not in a conscious way. I was longing for the creative, intuitive, sensual part of myself.

I have experienced both while writing this book. The animus part of me has wanted me to stay focused and meet deadlines but has separated me from my larger environment and even from my own well-being, while the anima has been opened to intuitive insights, has not wanted to be rushed for the sake of a deadline or perceived future accomplishment. My anima has wanted to stay connected with the beautiful nature around me, listening to the birds' song in the morning, enjoying my husband's company, and playing with our dog. It has wanted me to be fully alive, not just accomplished. This is exactly that part that edges us to investigate topics which are normally left unexplained, such as UFOs and the goddesses of ascension.

In a broader sense, the animus represents the materialistic, reductionist part of our science that tells us we are only the rational-logical part of our being which has no idea of higher levels of consciousness or of the existence of the anima. On the other hand, it represents the mystical, sensual part of our being that opens us to intuitive wisdom unknown to the rational mind. Alternatively, the animus is about competition, control, and purpose, while the anima is about connectedness, trust, and surrender. Without bringing animus and anima into some sort of agreement or harmony, there is little chance for true insight or balanced spirituality. I believe this corresponds to the third level in *The Gospel of Mary Magdalene* which deals with ignorance versus wisdom.

The final stage in Jung's model is the fulfilled self, which has reached the peak of its existence. Jung believed that the process was spiritual in nature and equated with self-realization. In *The Gospel of Mary Magdalene,* this is the fourth level, where we let go of the last vestiges of the ego.

What is the main lesson from Jung that is useful on our detective journey? It is that, to evolve, we must go within, work on ourselves, and integrate all of our parts. Without this, any ascension in consciousness is going to be temporary and we will descend again. This is something I have observed in many spiritual teachers. They reach a certain level, and then some unresolved attachment of the ego resurfaces. This is usually one of three things: money, fame, or sex. Because of the attachment, the teacher descends.

In other cases, it is the last whisper of ego, which I often experience in the form of a horrible sense of doubt that was also plaguing us at lower levels.

It is the "Who do you think you are?" in *The Gospel of Mary Magdalene*. "Do you think you can just write the book you want, and people will actually read it?" Or "Do you really want your academic colleagues to see your book on UFOs?"

As we close our detective work on Carl Jung and its connection to *The Gospel of Mary Magdalene*, I would like us to briefly go back to the person of Mary Magdalene. Although we cannot be certain about the physical existence of Inanna, Isis, and Demeter, I am convinced of the historical existence of Mary Magdalene.

Mary Magdalene is the conscious physical embodiment of a particular archetype pointing us in the direction of ascension. There is ample evidence for her existence and, indeed, of her having a special place in Jesus' circle. This is related in the Gnostic Gospels, which were not included in the Bible and include *The Gospel of Thomas*, *The Gospel of Philip*, and *The Gospel of Mary Magdalene*. The evidence for her existence and prominence is also a part of the accepted biblical tradition. Mary Magdalene is mentioned twelve times in the Bible, more than Matthew and Mark taken together. As a reminder of her importance, I would like to quote Mark 14:9: "Truly, I tell you, wherever the gospel is preached throughout the world, what she has done, will also be told, in memory of her."

It is especially painful to me that, after an attempt by the early Christian Church to demean Mary Magdalene as a prostitute, even some modern scholars are bent on banning her from our collective consciousness and argue that she did not exist. For those interested in my arguments for the existence of Mary Magdalene, I discuss other possibilities for her existence after the event of the Crucifixion in *The Other Goddess*.

I believe that Mary Magdalene was an especially significant embodiment of the same archetype as Inanna and Demeter. Her teachings focus on the upward movement of consciousness, which we now call ascension, and warn about choices that could lead to a descent. The teachings of *The Gospel of*

Mary Magdalene, although still encoded, are also the clearest. The myths of Inanna, Isis, and Demeter focus primarily on the descent and are told in the form of myth, while *The Gospel of Mary Magdalene* focuses more on the actual tools and less on the mythological story.

Now that we have arrived at the end of this part of our detective journey, in the next chapter, I will apply all four levels of ascension to deconstruct the state of mind of the creators of AI and their belief systems.

THE GOSPEL OF MARY MAGDALENE: UFOS AND AI

At each of the four levels in *The Gospel of Mary Magdalene* there is a choice to ascend or to descend. In my evaluation of the state of consciousness of at least some of the most visible creators of AI, they have chosen movement towards descent at each level.

At the first level, they chose wrong identification. This is identification with the material aspects of life, such as the idea that we are only physical beings and our minds equal our brain, which is simply some gray matter with a limited capacity to compute. This is why the creators of AI believe that we are just "water sacks" with limited minds.

At the second level, they chose wrong desire—to extend our physical existence through robotics by potentially sacrificing our ability for spiritual growth, transcendence, and ascension.

At the third level, they chose wrong understanding, believing that intelligence, especially mathematical-logical intelligence, is all that there is to consciousness, while forgetting that emotions, compassion, intuition, the ability to grow spiritually, and the ability to perceive and create beauty are also part of consciousness.

At the fourth level, they chose the voice of the ego rather than the purification of lower energies and creating from an expanded state of consciousness.

In contrast, had they chosen the higher aspects of each of the four levels of ascension in *The Gospel of Mary Magdalene*, they would have created from a very different space.

At the first level, they would have chosen right identification, which comes from turning within and fulfilling our human potential first.

At the second level, they would have chosen right desire. This is the desire for transcendence through both biological and spiritual means and which, in turn, leads to expanded states of consciousness that connect us not to some limited concept of intelligence but to Consciousness itself, which expands beyond logic and mathematics.

At the third level, they would choose wisdom instead of information, which they have understood as mere data by implanting a chip in our minds. True wisdom is available to us from within, not through external means.

At the fourth level, they would have purified the lower energies of the ego. In this way, their creations would come from a transcendental space of goodness rather than from egoic energies. Interestingly, in the Gnostic tradition from which *The Gospel of Mary Magdalene* comes, there exists the concept of the *demiurge,* a pretender god who creates from the lower energies of manipulation, causing chaos and confusion that, in turn, helps keep humans and all creation subservient to him.

If AI is created from the lower aspects of consciousness, then by default, it becomes an *egregore*—an entity that is potentially malevolent. At the same time, if AI had been created from a heightened state of consciousness, then it would have ethereal, not guileful, qualities. Consequently, it is not AI that might be problematic, but rather the state of mind and intentionality of the creators of AI.

As far as our investigation of *The Gospel of Mary Magdalene* and its methods of achieving higher levels of consciousness with respect to UFOs/UAPs goes, the most significant lesson is that from the third level of the ascension of consciousness. This is the level where the *Gospel* focuses on *nous*, which is our natural ability to stretch our field of perceptions. It is where the realm of the unusual but also the miraculous is manifest. In the context of *The Gospel of Mary Magdalene*, those who have access to this level of consciousness, as she did, are "blessed" because they can perceive what others cannot. I think this is a very positive and encouraging explanation, as it really is up to us whether we can experience the anomalous or not.

In simple language, we have the ability to be open-minded and present enough to see the marvelous world around us and within us. Esoteric traditions teach us that the delineation between what is within and what is without is superficial, and at higher levels of consciousness, it is nonexistent. The inner and outer world are one.

I am convinced that many instances of UFOs/UAPs are multidimensional phenomena and that whoever "they" are, and if "they" are truly more advanced than us, they would use consciousness rather than technology in the form of a spacecraft to reach us. It is up to us to reach out to the higher levels of our consciousness which are not only available to us but are also a part of our inner essence. And if we choose to connect with them, we have to allow for our *nous* to open the doors of perception for us—and this is what *The Gospel of Mary Magdalene* can help us with.

ESCAPING THE TRAP: PISTIS SOPHIA

T he next major text related to goddess mythologies that we will explore in our detective work is *Pistis Sophia*. I have personally encountered many surprises while studying the *Pistis Sophia* and I will share them in this chapter. One and the most significant surprise in *Pistis Sophia* is the theme of escaping a trap which was set up for us by the lower energies that are envious of our potential and our closeness to Source.

The other surprise is that there is very little information about every aspect of the text. Even its history seems to be largely a mystery, but we do know *Pistis Sophia* is a Gnostic text that was discovered in Egypt in 1773. Yes, in Egypt—just like *The Gospel of Mary Magdalene*. In 1785, the text was bought by the British Museum from the family of Dr. Anthony Askew, and for that reason, its designated name is the "Askew Codex." There is some evidence Dr. Askew bought *Pistis Sophia* from a bookseller in London for no more than ten pounds.

The physical part of the text is a parchment of 178 leaves, roughly equal to 356 pages, which makes it the longest text we have investigated here.

Although we do not know who authored *Pistis Sophia*, we have a poignant piece of information about the scribes who copied it. In the introduction to the text, its translator, G.R.S Mead, mentions that *Pistis Sophia* was copied from an older version of the text by two different scribes who used two different types of handwriting: one neat and careful and the other a bit shaky. Scholars have assumed that the scribe with a shaky hand was an old man.

Just as an aside, it always astounds me how traditional scholars habitually assume that all ancient texts had to be written or even copied by a man. In the case of *Pistis Sophia*, I think this assumption is especially doubtful, as the centerpiece of the text focuses on the main heroine (Pistis Sophia), and many questions are asked in the text by female disciples: Mary Magdalene, Martha, Mother Mary, and Salome. Indeed, Mary Magdalene asks thirty-nine questions in the text, which in itself shows her influence in the circle of disciples. Peter, Andrew, Philip, James, John, Matthew, and Simon also get their turn, but from the point of view of our investigation, the fact that female disciples are there, asking questions of Jesus and being praised by him, is significant.

This makes me wonder whether the people who wrote or copied this text could also have been women. My idea is not necessarily an isolated one. Although I have not heard of anyone else suggesting *Pistis Sophia* could possibly have been authored or preserved by women, Stevan L. Davies has argued that other Gnostic texts from the same period, such as "The Apocryphal Acts of the Apostles" were written by women. In his book, *The Revolt of the Widows: The Social World of the Apocryphal Acts of the Apostles* (2012), Davies explains his reasoning by giving examples of stories included which often focused on women taking charge of their spiritual and personal lives. The same could be true of *Pistis Sophia*.

The Askew Codex is written in Coptic but, as with many other Gnostic texts, there is a consensus that the current Coptic version was translated from Greek, the language in which *Pistis Sophia* was originally written. Again, as is usual in this kind of unclear situation, there are several theories as to when the text was first written. Dating varies from the first century CE to the fourth century CE, depending on which side of the Gnostic debate a scholar happens to be. Personally, I find Mead's translation of *Pistis Sophia* tedious to read, as it uses the same archaic vocabulary that is often seen in various editions of the Bible. From the point of view of a seeker, this only further obscures the already difficult text. While dealing with this challenge, it is good to remember that Mead was working on this translation during the 1890s, which was a time when this kind of style was preferred for sacred texts.

Now, let's look at the content of *Pistis Sophia* itself, as it takes the reader on a wild ride.

The main narrative focuses on Jesus' conversations with his disciples when he comes to stay with them for eleven years after the Resurrection. Therefore, this is an alternative storyline, so to speak, for Jesus and his disciples. Jesus gives esoteric teachings to his disciples: first lower-level revelations and then higher-level revelations. The whole text of *Pistis Sophia* is divided into six books and has a total of 148 chapters.

We will not be investigating this long, complex, and arcane text in all its detail. We will focus only on chapters 28 to 82, which describe Jesus' encounters with Sophia. As Jesus recounts the story of Sophia, the disciples pose questions or offer their own takes on the story, usually referring to Psalms or Odes of Solomon—most likely in an attempt to adjust the story to biblical standards. We will not be discussing their interpretations here. Instead, we will turn to the descriptions of the descent and ascent of Sophia, as we have done with other goddesses.

Broadly speaking, *Pistis Sophia*, narrated in Jesus' words, recounts his travels through hierarchically arranged *aeons*. The esoteric meaning of an aeon is that of an emanation of the Divine. In many philosophical traditions of late Antiquity, roughly from the first to the fourth century CE, the Universe is a spiritual place with aeons descending from the Divine Source to the lowest and darkest regions most removed from the Divine Light. Metaphorically speaking, the Universe is seen as a fountain of beings descending from and ascending back to the Source. In more modern parlance, I am tempted to call these aeons dimensions—as, just like dimensions, they are regions of subtle worlds, some more and others less evolved than humanity. Throughout *Pistis Sophia*, Jesus describes how, after the Resurrection, he moves between the twenty-four existing aeons. He describes his experiences along the way.

From a spiritual point of view, it is fascinating to learn that, as Jesus describes his arrival at each level he first sees their "veils," which "drew apart of their own accord" once they detected his presence and then "opened up" for him. This very much reminds us of the levels of ascension in other texts we have investigated here, and especially in *The Gospel of Mary Magdalene*— except in *The Gospel of Mary Magdalene,* we are told about inner obstacles we need to overcome and the choices we need to make to ascend to another level.

In *Pistis Sophia*, the rulers of the aeons appear to be external entities who allow Jesus to pass into their regions, but only after they recognize the "light vesture" he has within him. Then they have no choice but to reluctantly part the veils for him. This speaks of his high attainment, which even the rulers of the different aeons cannot resist. Thus, in *Pistis Sophia,* both Sophia and Jesus are faced with "rulers" who guard, and often obstruct, the process of ascension. In the same way as the gatekeepers, judges, and *gallas,* as demonic imposters, did in *The Descent of Inanna*, or through the use of other tricks such as the pomegranate seeds that obstruct Persephone's ascent in the *Homeric Hymn to Demeter*. This suggests that ascension is not only a challenging process but also includes significant obstacles to its achievement.

As Jesus moves through the hierarchy of aeons, he eventually ascends to the 13th Aeon where he encounters Pistis Sophia. She is trapped there "all alone...grieving and mourning" because she is not allowed to enter the aeon and its higher regions, even though this is her birthright. Sophia immediately recognizes the light of Jesus, which reminds her of the light she once possessed. And this is where the story gets interesting.

We are told that Sophia has lost access to her own light because of "self-willed" torments. She has willed these on herself because she has allowed herself to be tempted by false lights below her, believing they were higher than her own light. Even worse, she has mistaken the false lights below her to be the Highest Light. She has been led to believe that the light below her, and therefore clearly lower than herself, is the light of the Divine. She has allowed herself to be fooled by something less than herself.

At this point of the narrative, it is not clear if Jesus even wants to continue to tell the story of Sophia, as she is only one of many beings he encounters on his journey of ascension. It is Mary Magdalene who implores him to tell us the full story of Sophia. Mary Magdalene asks the very important question: How is it that Sophia, who herself is the highest emanation of the twenty-four possible emanations, was not allowed in to her own region? Mary Magdalene asks for more details because she wants to understand how it is possible for a highly evolved emanation of the Divine to fall so low to not be able to access her rightful place among the beings of light.

Jesus obliges Mary Magdalene and continues the story of Sophia with these words: "It came to pass, when Sophia was in the 13th Aeon..." she noticed the "veil of Treasury of the Light" above her. In other words, here Sophia has become aware of the Highest Light and "longed to reach" it[19]. She wants to be at the highest level of ascension and join with the Highest Light. She wants to be one with the Divine.

However, as she longs to move to the highest region of light, she stops to perform the mysteries of her own region, located in the 13th Aeon. It is not clear what these mysteries are exactly, but somehow, the rulers of the twelve aeons below her needed her to perform the mysteries so they would not be cut off from her light. As she continues to be absorbed in longing for the highest regions of light, the rulers of the lower regions start to hate her. They do so not only because she has stopped caring for them, but also because she desires heights that are not attainable for them. They hate her because she wants to ascend higher.

The rulers of the twelve regions below Sophia become so enraged at her that they decide to take revenge on her. First, they unite their efforts against her and pour all their power into one lower ruler, who is referred to as "the great triple-powered self-willed" as well as "lion-faced power." Then they strengthen their power by coercing the guards of her region to hate her as well. Their goal is not only to stop her from ascending, but also to banish her from her own region and bring her down to the lower regions, so she will have to remain obedient to them.

Sophia is so focused on her longing for the Highest Light that the only way the lower powers can bring her down is to deceive her. Slowly and surely, they manage to convince her that the lower emanation of the lion-faced ruler is the actual light she is longing for.

Their method of persuasion eventually works. One day, Sophia looks down at the regions of light below her and begins descending, believing that she is ascending. She thinks she is evolving, when in fact she is not only losing all her power and light but is descending into darkness and chaos.

What happens next sounds hauntingly familiar. Sophia descends to the level of the human condition. The lion-faced ruler "squeezed all the light powers" out of Sophia. He "cleaned out her light and devoured it, and her matter was thrust into chaos." In simpler words, the lower rulers strip her of her light and feed on her light, and through the light stolen from her, they become stronger. They then invest their power in an evil imposter who pretends to be the Creator but is not.

As we can imagine, after this brutal treatment of Sophia's light, Sophia is so exhausted that she has no strength to oppose the lion-faced imposter-ruler as he continues to suck all light from her and burden her with all the material powers that he controls. By the end of chapter 31, Sophia is completely lost in the material world, limited by its rigid rules, and disempowered. She has lost all her strength to fight and has reached rock bottom.

As in previous stories of goddesses' fates that we have investigated, Sophia is now stuck in the lower, material regions of existence and at the mercy of beings lower than herself. However, she remembers who she is, and remembers her rightful place in the order of the Cosmos, even if she does not feel she can do much about her current situation. Her only hope now is the Light of Lights, which she knows is the highest in the hierarchy of being and can save her. This extremely important but often forgotten part of *Pistis Sophia* is the knowledge that a higher power, higher than any material creation, exists to help her to survive and eventually ascend.

From chapter 32 on, she continually appeals to the Highest Light for help, even though her pleading for help goes unanswered. She is alone in her captivity and despair. Although she is cut off from all light, she keeps explaining to the Highest Light why she has fallen: "I have done this in my innocence," she keeps pleading, thinking that the "lion-faced power belonged to thee." By now, the rulers of the lower material realms not only oppress and torment Sophia, but also mock her while, at the same time, enjoying the power they have stolen from her.

Her pleas for help are repeated through chapter 82, with various versions of the same plea: "Save me out of the matter of this darkness, that I may not be submerged therein."

However, something very interesting has occurred by the end of chapter 32, when Sophia for the first time speaks of her "pair"—another being somehow related to her, "that he should come and save me." Later, we learn that her "pair" is none other than the Gnostic Jesus. She waits for him to descend to the chaos of matter and save her.

In chapter 35, Sophia realizes that, even though she had thought she could not fall any lower, something terrible has happened to her again. She notices that she has now become the same as the rulers of chaos. She partakes in their darkness. She learns the price of becoming a fully and utterly material creation without a soul. The remains of the Spirit that lived in her have abandoned her. She now has no spirit and sees no light. But, again, she holds on to her memory of the Highest Light and of her own light. And her pleading changes in tone slightly.

She speaks less of seeking revenge on the rulers of chaos, and instead prays for whatever is still left of her previous glory to continue to trust in the light while she remains in darkness. For reasons not explained in *Pistis Sophia*, Sophia's prayers are not answered for a very long time, and she has to endure more torments and mocking from the rulers of chaos. Yet she persists in asking for help and guidance from the light, which she now only vaguely remembers. She does this despite now living in fear, something she had never known before, and in the knowledge that her focus on light and her desire to move beyond darkness might offend the powers of chaos, who might punish and torment her even more.

Eventually, in chapter 47, Jesus takes pity on her and moves her to a more "spacious" region within the chaos. Although Sophia is still living in the realm of chaos and does not know that her "pair" (Jesus) is already helping her, her torments decrease a little. For the next several chapters, there is a game of hide and seek between the powers of chaos and Jesus. As Jesus gradually moves her to less horrid places in the realm of chaos and darkness, each time, the lion-faced ruler finds her and torments her, this time more as a form of punishment for attempting to escape his control.

In chapter 52, Sophia's pleas are finally accepted, and Jesus is sent to help her in a more direct way. The explanation for this help is meaningful for our investigation because, by this stage, Sophia has accepted two very important things. One is that she fully acknowledges that she was deluded by trusting something lower than herself to try to be better. The second thing is that, through her misery of being trapped in the realms of chaos, she has not given in to any other delusions. She has learned her lessons and refuses to be fooled again by things lower than herself.

Jesus, like a secret agent, advances towards Sophia in the midst of the rulers of chaos without any of them realizing who he is and why he is there. Eventually, Sophia recognizes Jesus and asks him to save her from the "crafty traps" of the rulers of chaos. In chapter 54, Sophia poses two interesting questions that we all ask of ourselves: Why does evil have so much "mighty power"? And why do the rulers of chaos choose to stay in darkness?

The answer to the first question is indirect and refers to our own willingness to give up our light and power. The answer to the second question is provided directly in chapter 55: The rulers of the lower regions prefer to stay in darkness because they love the chaos, so they are left to "abide there." In other words, they do not desire to ascend but rather prefer to manipulate the light of other beings for their own dark purposes.

By the end of the chapter, Sophia shares another insight with us: Her terrible descent has reaped something positive for everyone, as now we know that the rulers of chaos exist and, as a result, they will not be able to hide from us anymore. This is made possible only because Sophia has descended and is forced to see them for what they are.

The fight for Sophia's liberation continues up until chapter 82, with Jesus craftily moving her up the ladder of chaos. This is a tormenting climb for Sophia—the higher she is moved, the more furious the rulers of chaos are. In chapter 59, Jesus decides to create "a light-wreath" around her head so the rulers of the lower realms "could not have dominion over her." Through the power of the light around her head, Sophia's whole being is purified and she will no longer be influenced or tempted by the rulers of chaos.

If, for a moment, we consult other esoteric traditions, the light around her head might be interpreted as intuitive and uninterrupted access to higher wisdom, which helps her to discern the higher from the lower truths. In Hinduism, this would refer to the top two chakras, while in *The Gospel of*

Mary Magdalene, it would refer to *nous,* which acts as a transmitter to the realms of Pure Spirit.

Gradually and painfully, Sophia is led out of chaos, but not without many more torments and not without additional help. Not only Jesus, but also the Archangels Michael and Gabriel come to her side to help Sophia fight her way out of darkness. In this process, Sophia's heavenly helpers, with their incredible warrior might, manage to take away the light from the rulers of chaos that they have stolen from her.

Once the rulers of chaos see Sophia in her full light again, they dispatch Adamas the Tyrant and many other emanations of evil to surround Sophia in final attempts to prevent her ascension. But it is all in vain, because by now Sophia "took great courage," "was no longer in fear," and "did not tremble at the demon power of Adamas." Instead, she finds a new power in her own light and shines her light so strongly on her adversaries that "they fell one on another." For her courageous stand against the evil rulers and through abandoning all fear, Sophia is granted a "song of light" that will forever protect her from the rulers of chaos.

By chapter 76, Sophia is so strong and so full of light and wisdom that she is granted the power to move freely up and down the aeons—the lower and upper realms—without harm. Yet strangely, she is told that the struggle is not over yet and that the rulers of chaos will attempt to take her down three more times. Therefore, Sophia must stay grounded in her own light to be able to fight them off three more times. Chapter 82 completes the story of Sophia in *Pistis Sophia.*

In our investigative journey, we cannot help but notice similarities between *The Descent of Inanna,* the *Homeric Hymn to Demeter,* *The Gospel of Mary Magdalene,* and *Pistis Sophia.* The similarities are most obvious in the storytelling itself, as each of the heroines/goddesses face similar challenges. In each case, they are pulled down to the lower realms by some form of trickery and are trapped there until help arrives in the form of other beings who understand the significance of the presence of the goddess in the world. These beings then conspire in their rescue. In *Pistis Sophia*, Sophia descends unaware that entities less powerful and less glorious than herself have conspired against her because they envy her light and her desire to ascend and reach the Highest Light.

As a result, while Sophia is descending, she is still convinced she is ascending, until it is too late. In *The Descent of Inanna*, the Goddess Inanna believes she is simply attending the funeral of her sister's husband. In a similar fashion, she has no idea that she will be asked to give up all her powers and not be allowed to return to her kingdom "high above." In the *Homeric Hymn to Demeter*, Demeter's daughter Persephone is snatched away without her permission while admiring a beautiful flower. *The Gospel of Mary Magdalene* is the only text not to discuss a story of a personal descent but explains the whole process of descent and ascent in general terms that are applicable to every soul and every being. *The Gospel of Mary Magdalene* makes sure we understand that this is not an isolated story of one goddess or another, but rather that it has universal application. The *Gospel* teaches us that this is everyone's story.

In all the texts investigated here, each goddess/ heroine has helpers. In the case of *The Descent of Inanna*, it is her faithful servant, Ninshubur, who is the memory of her true glory. She manages to gather support for her journey back upwards. In the *Homeric Hymn to Demeter*, it is the Goddess Hecate and the God Helios who provide Demeter with clues about her daughter's fate. In *Pistis Sophia*, a Christian element appears, as it is the grace of Jesus as well as of the Archangels Gabriel and Michael that aids her ascension. In *The Gospel of Mary Magdalene,* it is the teachings Mary Magdalene provides that can assist everyone in the process of ascension.

Although all the myths that we have investigated here deal with malicious and envious rulers of the lower realm, the evil rulers are explicitly named in *Pistis Sophia*. They are "the tyrants that became as the dead," who "all lost power and fell down to the ground in their aeons and became as the dead world-dwellers with no breath in them." This is an extremely powerful description of these rulers, and it reminds me a lot of other stories, including biblical ones, of fallen angels that malign humanity. They are "as the dead" but somehow still functioning and their operations depend on feeding upon the light of ascending human beings. Even more so, in *Pistis Sophia*, the rulers are not only evil and fallen but are also envious of the human power to ascend, so they do everything in their power to deceive us.

It is my interpretation that it is not humanity itself that these rulers want to destroy, but rather the innate human ability to ascend to the light and the highest realms from which the rulers are banned. This human ability comes with what is called *nous* in *The Gospel of Mary Magdalene*—our sacred faculty to be one with the Highest Light and to achieve our own Divinity.

I have no doubt that, in each case, the Goddess who represents our unique and holistic way of perceiving light is the rulers' greatest fear. The Goddess represents the other means of knowing that threatens the fallen rulers, which is why they have to push her to the margins and ridicule her wisdom as unscientific or not factual. It is precisely this kind of wisdom that the rulers want to control. It is the Goddess, known as Pistis Sophia or Faith-Wisdom, whom they want to destroy.

At the same time, these rulers are not always external to us. The rulers we can control are within us. As the esoteric adage says, "What is above, is below, what is within, is without." The "what is within" is the most spiritually significant part here and it is the only part that we can truly control. This is also the part that means we can freely ascend. No one can stop us—unless, of course, we allow ourselves to be distracted.

Why do we allow ourselves to be distracted? Because distraction is an easier path. Indeed, this is not a path at all but a way of constant unconscious submission. It is so much easier to blame the situation in which humanity finds itself on external influences—and they are there, for certain. But complaining and pointing fingers has never changed anything and never will change anything. Neither will waiting for an advanced alien race to come and save us which is a popular narrative nowadays. Why not? There is only one simple answer to this question: ascension is an inner task. No one else can do this for us.

All the mystery traditions teach us that we must change from within. We have to transform how we think of ourselves and what choices we make, one step at a time, just as *The Gospel of Mary Magdalene* teaches us. One level at a time. We fall and we get up. We make a stupid decision, we learn our lesson, and we make a different choice next time. This is precisely why similar challenging situations occur in our lives over and over again—to give us the opportunity to make a different choice, to choose a higher and more conscious path. This starts with the vision of ourselves that we hold. Do we see ourselves as beings filled with Divine potential, or do we see ourselves without power? We all have to ask ourselves this question and, based on our answer, we need to make new choices about how we envision ourselves.

When faced with a decision, we each need to ask: What would the best version of myself do? And we need to try our hardest to do just that. Then, and only then, will the external circumstances change.

I have learned a painful lesson: Trying to change external circumstances is a never-ending game. The true shift does not come by a constant rearrangement of external pieces but through inner change. Anyone who has left a job or a relationship because of politics or toxicity—which might be real—has very quickly found themselves in similar circumstances again, but in another workplace or another relationship. Nothing changes until we change from within. Ascension, transcendence, and transformation is primarily an inner job. It really is worth trying.

The good news is that we are not alone on this journey. As with all the goddesses we have investigated here, we have helpers and guides and knowledge from those who have taken the path before us. They often appear when we lose all hope, because it is at that point that our being cracks open. We surrender to something new, to a new form of wisdom or a way out that is offered to us from a source that perhaps, in the past, we would not have accepted.

In our detective work, all the goddesses have gone through the descent, and they have all returned to their rightful place: the highest versions of themselves. Collectively, we are at a crossroads, but we have the guidance of sacred texts and myths. They are our sacred memory, and they are our treasury of remembrance of what is possible for us. They remind us that, at some stage, our consciousness descended and became caught in the lower regions without light. These stories are cautionary as well. They teach us not to be deceived by what is lower than ourselves and to focus on regaining our place in the Universe.

What form of wisdom does the Goddess Sophia represent, spiritually and consciousness wise? In many ways, this is the question that makes the most sense in the stories of the descent and ascent of goddesses. What did they really descend from and where does their ascension path lead?

It is my conviction, after looking at different sacred texts and goddess-oriented mythologies, that the stories of the descent and ascent of the goddesses are stories of the descent and ascent of our own consciousness. Something has happened and we have forgotten who we are. We have forgotten our higher capacities and our natural connection to higher wisdom. I would like to emphasize here that when we speak of higher wisdom, I do not mean the type of knowledge that is logical, rational, or mechanical. I am not talking about knowledge based on information and engineering. I am not talking about the form of knowledge that the materialistic science of our times excels at. As impressive as it might be, the engineering knowledge of modern techno-lords is not wisdom, and it is not and never will be a path to ascension. This kind of knowledge was coined *techne* in ancient Greece. It can be useful, but it is not wisdom.

In fact, after studying *Pistis Sophia*, I have come to believe that the techne offered by many proponents of AI is precisely the false light that Sophia saw. Let's not forget that it was her own delusion that led her to her descent. We have to be very aware that her descent was not intentional; she truly believed that she was ascending. She believed that the false light she saw was the ultimate Divine Light.

Unfortunately for her, once she realized that she had been deluded, that she had mistaken the false light for her salvation, it was too late. She was trapped in the lower realms of artificial matter and all she could do was let the evil rulers torture and degrade her even more, because she had lost all her own natural light. All she could do was cry for help in the darkness. Her descent was so complete and her desperation so emotionally disturbing that we can identify with her pain and despair.

However, the story of Sophia is not about us feeling compassion for her. It is a warning for us. It is a warning that this is what will happen to us if we believe the false light. This false light may have different forms in different epochs. In our times, it is the belief that Artificial Intelligence will save us, that it will cure disease and give us immortality. This is the false light we are facing now. The story of Sophia and the myths of Inanna and Demeter are not there for our entertainment, but to repeat the same warning. The geographical locations and dating change, whilst the warning remains the same: Don't become seduced by false light and its promises.

Fortunately for us, all these stories have a second part. In each of these myths the goddess finds her way back. Yes, she has been tricked. Yes, in Sophia's case, the evil rulers jealous of her natural light have taken advantage of her desire to be eternal—but with a little help from higher regions, she begins her ascension back to her rightful place in the cosmos and she reclaims her true light and power.

Perhaps because I love *The Gospel of Mary Magdalene*, I am inclined to believe that the path to ascension is best depicted and described there, as this sacred text gives us the actual tools to ascend. It is easy to dismiss the tools it is offering because they do not belong to the world of the techne. They are our inner tools, and no one, not even the evil rulers, can take our inner power and inner tools from us. However, these tools can be used only if we remember that we have them and that they are always at our disposal. That is why Ninshubur in *The Descent of Inanna* plays such a crucial role. She is Inanna's memory. She awakens the higher realm to her situation and help eventually comes. In the *Homeric Hymn to Demeter*, it is Demeter who remembers and persists in saving her daughter, Persephone. In *Pistis Sophia,* it is the Gnostic version of Jesus who comes to Sophia's help.

This wisdom is different from the information-based knowledge to which we are conditioned Although pushed to the side, it has survived in many spiritual traditions, and it has often been represented by Sophia (meaning wisdom in Greek). It has persisted under many names in various theologies. For example, in Christianity it survived as the Holy Sophia, who was a part of the Holy Trinity. Only later was Sophia neutered when the Bible was translated into Latin. In her Latinized version, she became the Holy Spirit.

In Hinduism, she is known as the *buddhi*—the higher intellect that grasps spiritual understanding outside the realm available to reason and logic. In Zen Buddhism, there is the concept of *satori*, the same immediate knowing that defies logic and yet knows everything all at once. Even in Christian theology, Thomas Aquinas spoke *intellection* again another form of Sophia, which embodies the sudden and full understanding of higher truths.

Thus, *Pistis Sophia* is both the story of escaping the trap of deceitful lower energies and a warning of what happens to us when we do surrender to them. Fortunately for us, Sophia's escape was successful, and we can benefit from her lessons and the form of wisdom she has come to represent. According to the goddess-centered myths and sacred texts, this form of wisdom is our greatest treasure. I think we can safely argue that what is commonly known as "intuition" is the same as Wisdom-Sophia. It is our "Treasury of the Light," and we need to stay vigilant so that we do not exchange this for the lower light of the creators of Artificial Intelligence. I am convinced that at least some of the UFO phenomena, often identified as the White Lady or other radiant beings, might have referred to just that.

I believe that the recovery of this now "alien" form of wisdom is essential, not only for our evolution, but for our very survival. It teaches us, over and over again, that spiritual ascension is the best way of creating change individually and collectively. It opens for us the possibility of infinite growth. Without that wisdom, which I call Goddess Consciousness, we are capable of survival, reasoning, and action, but we lack insight, intuition, and emotion. At the same time, if we choose to partake in that wisdom, we open our minds to the possibility of our own greatness, which is our birthright and is waiting to be accessed and activated by our choices.

Is this possibility still open to us?

THE END IS THE BEGINNING: BABA YAGA

T his exasperating presence had a familiar feel to it. And it was not an "it"; it was a "she," in her embodiment as Baba Yaga. As everything is connected in our existence—whether we want to admit it or not, Baba Yaga also had a personal matter to discuss with me. I had to accept where I came from, even if, and especially if, I did not care about my roots, as I have always considered myself a vagabond and a citizen of the planet—if such identification is ever required. Baba Yaga's presence was familiar to me with her general annoyance (which perfectly matched my own) and impossible insistence. She would simply not take no for an answer, as I remembered from our first encounter.

About a year ago, when I was exhausted after writing and promoting another book, I lay down on my bed and called upon the goddesses whom I had written about in that book. I called upon Ninmah, I called upon Inanna, Isis, Mary Magdalene, and Sophia to come to my rescue, to heal me and to guide me. As I was calling upon their names, another ancient goddess showed up—and she had a good laugh looking at my misery. It was the Slavic trickster Goddess, Baba Yaga. I was startled because I had not called upon her and was surprised because I am disconnected from my geographical origins, given that, by choice, I've lived most of my life elsewhere.

Instantly, I was transported to her hut in an old forest. It was exactly as I had always remembered it: both strangely familiar and belonging to another old, forgotten world. The hut was lost in the old forest. It stood above the ground supported by one monstrously large chicken leg and kept spinning: gently, when Baba Yaga was in a friendly mood, and quickly when she was annoyed.

We were both inside the hut where she was cooking a fragrant soup with herbs in a large cauldron over the fire. I was lying on a bed made of some sticks and rags. She was listening to my self-pity and fear while continually stirring the cauldron, murmuring to herself and moving around her hut. We communicated and understood each other without words. As I whined, she was giggling, as if the stories I was telling her were as old as the world itself and, frankly, ridiculously boring! She was friendly, but not in a motherly way. I knew that at any moment she could turn into a monster if she decided to teach me a lesson. But for now, she was taking care of me.

A day later, my mom, who lives in Poland, called me. Without knowing of my experience from between the worlds with Baba Yaga, she told me that the day before, she had gone to visit a new friend who was introduced to her by a neighbor. The friend, an old lady, lives in a forest about an hour away by car from the city where my mother resides. The name of the forest is *Stary Las*, which translates into English as the Old Forest. My mom told me that she had been charmed by the woman, who lives in a wooden house in the surrounding forest. Years ago, the woman and her husband had bought a shack there and had made it into a little house. Her husband had died soon after, and since then, she had lived alone. She would tell her guests how much she loves the forest and her life.

Her daughter had bought her a small piece of land near the tiny house and the lady had planted wildflowers there to attract bees. She had found a local beekeeper who had taught her how to take care of her beehives and to collect honey. When my mom and her neighbor visited the woman, the woman treated them to a homemade tea mixed with local berries and her own honey. She served the tea in old porcelain teacups of rare beauty.

As they sipped the tea and ate cake, the woman told them that autumns were difficult there because of the constant rain and mud, but winters were magical, white and quiet. It was during the winters that a female deer and a female wild boar would come to visit, as if checking on her and letting her know they were still around. The woman's two dogs knew them and did not bark when they saw them.

My mom came back home to her apartment, as if spellbound by the experience. She called me to tell me about her visit. As she was telling me this, I had an immediate realization that the woman was another version of Baba Yaga. For centuries, many women have embodied this archetype, and I realized that through my mother's experience, Baba Yaga had reached out to me again.

We live in a world that is completely skewed, and anyone with any remembrance of their soul can feel in their gut that we are moving in the wrong direction. Artificial Intelligence has now been unleashed, and we know this is a turn we should not be taking. We are visited by other beings, either spiritual, interdimensional, or extraterrestrial—who continue to warn us about our choices. The whole mainstream narrative diverts our attention so we will not see what is truly going on—that we are being stripped of our souls and connection to nature.

It came to me that Baba Yaga has many faces. She is a trickster and shapeshifter, but she knows her soul. She knows her mission. She knows it is our connection with Nature and Spirit that is our destiny, and that this is where our spiritual evolution is meant to happen. We are the Baba Yagas— the ones who will keep telling the stories of our origin and the stories of our future in a different voice, from a different perspective.

Whatever happens, we need to remember that there is another narrative, another option, another choice. There is another way other than the one we are being offered at this moment. And I knew she wanted me to include her in our detective journey.

I set out on the search that she directed me on. Right from the beginning of the writing of this book, I knew I had to follow intuitive threads, as this is how Goddess wisdom works. If I wanted to write about this, I needed to practice it—and to practice it, I needed to trust Baba Yaga's guidance. Dutifully, I turned to a recent scholarly work written in Polish on the religions of the ancient Slavs, which was intended for seekers. The reason I will not cite the title or the author or even the date of publication here is that this book was a great disappointment to me. Just to be clear, it is well researched, but not only did it leave out the story of Baba Yaga herself, but also those of the many other Slavic goddesses. Just like many scholars before him, the author did not think it important to mention even one goddess in his book. This is the sole reason I will not name him here, as to name him would be unkind, even though I was tempted to do so.

For anyone born in Eastern Europe, Baba Yaga or Baba Jaga ("j" is pronounced "y" in Slavic languages) is a familiar figure. She is represented as an old woman, independent, living in the forest and somehow dangerous, capable of eating people or even children. She is often used by parents to scare their children into obedience: "If you don't do this, Baba Yaga will come and get you." In folk literature and scholarly evaluations, she is always shown as an ambiguous figure: fierce, even scary. This portrayal also comes with an acknowledgement that she has gifts to offer, such as the gift of transformation and healing, but it is well known that the fainthearted should stay away.

Baba Yaga has been given most attention by Russian scholars and Slavic fairytale collectors such as Mikhail Lomonosov, Alexander Afanasyev, Andrey Toporkov, and Vladimir Propp. Afanasyev believed that Baba Yaga's name comes from the proto-Slavic word *oz*, meaning the "serpent," which is very interesting. In many traditions, the serpent is an ambiguous figure, although most of the time it represents forbidden wisdom.

Lomonosov, who attempted to relate Slavic deities to the Roman gods, could not find an equivalent for Baba Yaga. There is no known category in the Roman Pantheon for her. She stands on her own. Propp concluded that Baba Yaga does not have a coherent image but is a collection of ancient stories. Toporkov argues that the physical attributes surrounding Baba Yaga, such as the pestle, were used in ancient Slavic rituals performed by women.

It really is telling how this figure representing woman's wisdom is both despised and feared by the societal establishment. She was made to be old and repulsive, with bony legs, and saggy breasts, and even her vulva is mentioned as being particularly offensive. For me, the last description is both sad and infuriating, as it shows how some parts of the masculine mind fear the very principle of life and its profound wisdom. And, essentially, how can we stay open to the wisdom offered by the feminine if we despise the very core of her?

I would like to take this even further. Baba Yaga has been used to instill a fear of feminine wisdom in all of us. A long time ago, someone decided that her wisdom was too dangerous for them, and so they banished her to the margins of our subconscious, where fear lies.

Knowing my mother had met an actual incarnation of Baba Yaga, I turned to my mother's connections, who recommended several sources, some in Polish and one in English. The source in English is *Baba Yaga. Slavic Earth Goddess* (2021) by Natalia Clarke. This is a personal, therapeutic, and poetic exploration of the old Slavic entity.

Many versions of her are like the pieces of a broken mirror of who she really is. Let's look through the broken pieces of that mirror.

Baba Yaga is also known as the Wicked Wood Nymph, the Forest Spirit, the Witch, the Energy, the Ruler of the Elements, the Wise Woman, and the Queen of the Afterlife. This last association, especially, is strangely reminiscent of her deeper past, as embodied in the goddesses who had to descend to the regions below to bring us the wisdom we need: Inanna, Demeter, Sophia and, in a more indirect way, Mary Magdalene.

In the opening of her book, Clarke assures us that Baba Yaga is not surprised by anything anymore because she has seen it all. The most striking statement Clarke makes about her version of Baba Yaga is that Baba Yaga's "food is her cells, both human and non-human" and that when she smells a human, she feels repulsed. This is something we need to investigate more closely. Why does Baba Yaga, who, at least traditionally, was considered the earthiest of all goddesses, possess cells that are both human and non-human? And why does she despise the smell of humans?

Nature as Non-Human Intelligence

Before we can fully answer these two questions, we need to answer another one: What does *non-human* mean here? Too often, we associate non-human intelligence with Artificial Intelligence. But surrounding us, in the natural world, is a deep and wise intelligence that is not human. If Simone, or Moon Lady, from Diana Pasulka's *Encounters* was my first brush with ignorance of higher truths, another interviewee in Pasulka's book was the opposite of that ignorance. That person's name is Iya Whitley. Like many of Pasulka's interviewees, Iya is a professional associated with the space program. She is a space psychologist and supports astronauts who work in extreme environments. She developed a "Psy-Matrix" that helps astronauts to "acclimate to new mental states and to the shock of new consciousness." [20]

Now, this is already incredibly interesting, but there is more to Iya than this. As we understand more about Iya's work, we also learn about what really happens to the consciousness of astronauts as they orbit the Earth. Apparently, astronauts develop a different form of consciousness, a type of astounding sense of unity with the whole of Earth, the whole of humanity, and the whole of life. In one instance, quoted in Pasulka's book, astronauts

216

at some stage could not perform normal duties for which they were trained because they were affected by the "fascinating, unprecedented" experience of floating in space. The state of their consciousness had expanded, and the simplest functions became difficult to perform.

I would like to pause here, as a similar expansion of consciousness can happen to many people who undergo a profound spiritual awakening. The very same thing happened to me at one point when I went through the formal initiation to an esoteric tradition, and then later again during an erotic tantric encounter: my consciousness expanded, and I saw the space around me first stretch in all directions and then contract around me. This led me to realize that our usual perceptions of both space and consciousness are in a contracted form and that worlds much vaster than our current one are open to us under the right conditions.

My experience is not unheard of, and many others have had similar experiences. Testimonies about the expansion of consciousness come from all spiritual traditions. This kind of ordeal is life changing. I use the word "ordeal" because after such experiences, nothing can ever be the same again and it is nearly impossible to return to what we consider "normal."

When I experienced my first expansion of consciousness, like the astronauts in Pasulka's book, I, too, was subsequently not able to perform basic functions, and was forced to stay in the bliss of complete unity with everything and that mysterious sense of unknowing or knowing not comprehended by the rational part of our minds. The fact that astronauts also experience this same shift in perception when in space is striking from the point of view of our detective work. They experience what all the myths of the descents and ascensions of the goddesses are telling us. As we have seen, all the goddesses underwent this contraction of consciousness when descending from above, then regained their expanded states as they ascended. This similarity cannot be ignored. Is it possible that when people are in a contracted state of consciousness, what appears to them as a spaceship could be the perception of another dimension or reality when they are in an expanded state?

Space psychology is Iya's day job. Her real passion is creating a cosmic language which will allow humanity to connect "with intelligences that surround all of us, globally and in the natural world.". And what form of knowing has Iya used to do this? Intuition. Iya explains, in Pasulka's *Encounters*, that she experiences "the Earth Consciousness as a pattern that ... through vibrations in sounds and visual forms in nature, is trying to reach out to us." [21]

Iya believes that all nature, both plants and animals, is sentient. This kind of belief is a form of spiritual philosophy to which I subscribe and is called pantheism. In pantheism, all creation is part of the Divine and no one being is better than another. The idea of the dominion of one species over another is simply ridiculous and untrue. Iya's goal is to reconnect us with the language of nature and the universe itself.

I see Iya as a rare species, as she embodies Goddess wisdom while using the tools of technology to bring her vision to realization. For me personally, Iya represents the deep wisdom that is alien to people who are so disconnected from the natural and intuitive world that they can only understand what is artificial.

Iya's work so clearly proves what many spiritual traditions have claimed for millennia—that there is a vast intelligence which that surrounds us every moment of our lives. This intelligence is in trees, in animals, in the air we breathe, and in the water we drink. It is in our dreams when we encounter different worlds. It is in all of our anomalous experiences, whether we label them as UFO sightings, interdimensional contacts, or spiritual awakenings. It is everywhere in the mythologies of the goddesses' descents and ascensions. And yet, many choose to ignore this vast intelligence, even suppress it, and instead praise those who create artificial forms of life.

I can relate to Iya's work because, through my own spiritual awakening, I have experienced the language she speaks of. It is no secret that in esoteric traditions, one is often granted a gift. In Hinduism, this gift is called a *siddhi*—a special ability—given to a willing disciple. I make no claims about possessing any of the great gifts; the ones I have been granted come and go depending on the state of my consciousness and shifting focus. But, if I am quiet and open, and willing to block out the noise of the rational mind and its fears, I *can* hear the trees speak to me. I can understand the deep wisdom of animals. At times I can even understand what they want to tell us in their gentle but constant whisper.

It is not animals, and it is not trees that need to evolve. It is we humans. We all, collectively, have been given the highest gift of Wisdom, represented in the goddess mythologies before they were corrupted by people who could not understand—people who called the forest goddesses and nymphs harlots and who invented the word "nymphomaniac," which only reflects the darkness of their own states of mind. People who changed the narratives of the lives of goddesses and their priestesses and called them prostitutes and evil doers. These people have confused us, and they continue to instill fear in us so that we do not have the time or confidence to hear the wisdom within us and around us. The good news is, we can choose what we want to listen to: to the whispers of nature and the goddesses—or to external, artificial noise. The choice is and always has been ours.

In many esoteric traditions, the cosmos is consciousness, and nothing that exists is devoid of it. The cosmos might possess a different form of consciousness than humans do, but it is still consciousness. Some of my favorite philosophers, such as Abhinavagupta or John Scotus Eriugena, speak of this. For Abhinavagupta, consciousness is not only present in everything, but it also predates physical manifestations. For Eriugena, cosmic creation is an elaborate cascade of beings, flowing first outwardly from Source and then inwardly back to its Divine Source. In modern times, Teilhard de Chardin spoke of the same process, with all creation traveling from an Alpha point to an Omega point, where all culminates as One.

The Alien Goddess?

But back to Baba Yaga and her non-human aspects which, I believe, refer to the vast intelligence of the natural world that permeates not only our planet but exists throughout the entire cosmos. Since Baba Yaga is full of contradictions and refuses to conform to a motherly, always sacrificial, tender femininity, we may have to seek our own experience of her, but this inner trip is not for the fainthearted. As Clarke says beautifully in her book, *Baba Yaga,* "She hears a deep cry within a human being," and will decide whether death or salvation will come to the one who has called upon her.

Clarke's encounters with Baba Yaga usually come in dreams. Outside of the realm of dreams, Clarke can sense her energy, "an elder presence." Clarke has also learned that her questions to Baba Yaga are only answered if she asks the right question at the right time and without fear. You have to be prepared for whatever Baba Yaga says, even if you do not like it. Otherwise, Baba Yaga is not interested.

My encounters with Baba Yaga have never been in the space of dreams but rather in that space of the imaginal or liminal when we are fully aware of our current reality but also present and aware of some unusual opening, something out of the ordinary. As I described at the beginning of the chapter, she came to me when I was lying in bed, exhausted, feeling sorry for myself and calling upon the goddesses about whom I had written previously: Ninmah, Inanna, Isis, Mary Magdalene, Kali, Sundari. But it was Baba Yaga who came. She flooded me with images of us together in her hut and with the distinct otherworldly presence that was her. She took care of me but also found my self-pity amusing and rather annoying. Yet she answered my call. Perhaps this had something to do with my Slavic roots. Perhaps she is too ancient to consider our roots.

There was an element of the unknowable about her intentions, in the sense that they could shift from the merciful to supreme annoyance. I had no knowledge of what she was planning to do with me. I often still feel her presence near the tall, spread-out eucalyptus tree close to our house. Sometimes I collect little twigs and branches fallen from the big tree, and as I thank the tree for its gifts, I offer them to Baba Yaga and place them in our special place by the fence. Somewhere deep within the ancient spaces of my memory, I know that she appreciates the gifts of nature, that she appreciates my understanding of the tree's offerings, rather than the raging of my neighbors about the mess the tree's leaves make.

I can also sense her in a little grove on a property which I pass by when walking our dog, Charlotte. I do not ask Baba Yaga for anything. I am only aware of her ancient presence, and as I am doing these little things, I can sense that her anger is really sadness: sadness at what has become of us and where we are heading. She is tired of coming to our rescue while we continue living with our arrogance and greed.

Clarke also surprised me with some new information about Baba Yaga: Three Horsemen follow her everywhere and are her guardians. Baba Yaga does not seem to me like someone who needs protection, but these guardians are there, ready to follow her orders, whatever they might be. My first association with this new information was negative: The Three Horsemen reminded me of the Four Horsemen of the Apocalypse: Conquest, Famine, War, and Death. They are, like Baba Yaga's Three Horsemen, represented by colors: white, red, black, and pale. What are these threatening figures, reduced in number to three, doing around Baba Yaga? Are they later, Christian additions, or have they always been around her? These questions are very difficult to answer. Academic scholarship about Baba Yaga is minimal and negative. The rest, as Propp discovered, are pieces of a familiar but ancient female figure that are scattered around in Slavic fairy tales from different ages.

Clarke does not ask these questions and instead gives her own interpretation. For Clarke, the Three Horsemen of Baba Yaga represent the sacred masculine, which, together with Baba Yaga, provides a balance to the cosmos. Clarke associates them with alchemical stages of transformation, where *negredo* (black) represents the dark night and dreamtime, *calcinatio* (red) stands for "burning time" and passion, and *solutio* (white) is for a new beginning. As with everything connected to Baba Yaga, the Three Horsemen are ambiguous figures and difficult to classify as either good or bad. I think Clarke's interpretation perhaps refuses to look closer at this ambiguity.

For our detective journey, this impossibility of a simple moral judgment about Baba Yaga and the Three Horsemen brings to mind the dilemmas of religious figures in other spiritual traditions who have been situated on the margins, such as, the figure of Sophia or the Tantric Kali, as well as the *shaktis*, *dakinis*, and *kapalikas*.

Kali, like Baba Yaga and Mary Magdalene, is portrayed with a skull. *Shaktis* and *dakinis* are powerful elemental entities that need to be appeased or at least acknowledged before Tantric rituals, as they can create havoc in the Universe if upset or ignored. They are like nature in that they give us life but also take it away. Sages have taught us for millennia about the powers of these entities and the need to be able to channel them into appropriate goals—ideally, for the sake of our own ascension. *Kapalikas* are radical Tantric practitioners who disobey social rules and worship the *shaktis*. What if they are neither good nor bad? What if, as all esoteric traditions teach us, they are mirrors to our souls and reflect to us who and what we are at any given moment? And what if it is entirely up to us how they manifest in our reality?

Perhaps the Four Horsemen of the Apocalypse and the Three Horsemen of Baba Yaga are the same. They mirror to us the world we have created and tell us when we have reached the end. Are they both harbingers of the end and the alchemical process for the new to be born? Do they end one process and begin the new?

Let's continue this journey of unveiling Baba Yaga and the Goddess Consciousness, whose wisdom we are seeking. My sources, which I obtained via the Baba Jaga, woman that my mom met in the Old Forest near her town, were Polish folklore researchers from the Lublin Skansen (Lublin Folk Museum). And among their work were articles from the Arbor Mundi site and two scholarly papers by Bogumila Dziel, an academic from the University of Silesia in Poland.

These set me on another realization. Apparently, Baba Yaga has not always been portrayed as an old and repulsive woman. She was also a nymph or a goddess of sacred rites who guided people to the Underworld. Some of the researchers link her to Persephone, Demeter's daughter. Others believe she is an ancient representation of the Great Mother, finding links to her in ancient Anatolia. Depending on the context, Baba Yaga can be seen as a young woman, as a mother, or as an old woman. Baba Yaga and her strange looking abode represent both initiation and the place of initiation. She was known as a healer, a goddess who knew magic and was not afraid to use it. The feared cauldron situated in the middle of her hut, where she supposedly cooks young men and women and even children, was originally a cauldron of purification and a place where evil was skillfully isolated so that it could not affect the goodness of the world. Sometime in her ancient history, she has been transformed into an old witch.

As I walk through that part of her story, yet another interpretation emerges from the liminal field of my consciousness, where every conceivability is stored. In that field where portals open for me, Baba Yaga chose the disguise of the old woman, though not initially. At first, she came to us in her full glory, young and beautiful and willing to share with us her sacred rites of ascension and evolution. She came to us as Inanna, as Isis, as Demeter, as Mary Magdalene, and as Sophia. She has come to us over and over again

223

in many disguises. But each time, we have chosen not to listen. Each time, either our own ignorance and greed or some external forces that do not want us to evolve, have tricked her into the darkness.

Each time, our ancient memory of her has brought her back to us in sacred stories, in fairy tales, or in rejected gospels. Each time, her wisdom has been pushed to the margins of our consciousness, and each time our arrogance has called her wisdom unscientific. And each time, she has come to remind us that the place of power comes from *nous*—that space of dreams and imagination.

She has asked us repeatedly to choose ascension through Spirit, and each time we have chosen to rule over others. And this time, when she saw that we have chosen technology over Spirit, she turned within and hid in her sacred darkness. She was forgotten and concealed into mythical accounts, waiting for the final call again. And, as before and so now, she will end what needs to be ended so that a new cycle can be born.

As we have not learned much.

Recently, I had my own third and so far, final encounter with Her. She came to me in that space of heightened awareness between the night and the dawn and wearily showed me a vision that was strangely familiar to both of us, as this has happened before and is going to happen again.

A portal of *nous* opens again and, for a moment, two dimensions collapse into one. From a gleaming orb, a hybrid being, half human, half machine, comes out to find Her. Its body has become hard and machine-like. With it comes another creature: its robotic child created by the hybrid's mind.

The robotic child does not understand why there is no meaning within its being.

The hybrid only knows that it is she-the-mother to its child.

They have traveled together for so long through the emptiness of space, but they cannot see or hear the infinite life song of the cosmos.

The ground around them is barren, devoid of trees and flowers. There is no birdsong welcoming them in the morning and there are no butterflies dancing among them. The waters are dark and defiled and the air is barely breathable.

Is there a soul in their shells?

Outside Her dwelling, they tell Her their story, a story of how they have traveled through time to find Her. They beg Her for help because now they know they have listened to the voices of deception, which were designed to mislead them.

She knows she is an alien goddess for them because they have disconnected from what is truly theirs: the gift of ascension that all sacred texts have been teaching them for millennia. They do not understand that their own greatness lives within their souls and that they can always connect with her in the space of the *nous*—the third space between the physical and spiritual, where imaginal possibilities have always waited for them. She knows it is ignorance of that wisdom which has led them to the place of destruction again.

She is too ancient to ask herself again about the force that pushes humans towards their own demise. Is it the impulse to create without consequences? Or is it a hidden sense of inferiority that leads them to create what they falsely believe is higher than them?

There is too much pain in Her being. So much hope lost and so much potential overlooked. She wants to turn away from them and end the cycles of time forever.

If only they can stop looking outside of themselves for answers and hear the heartbeat of their own bodies and feel the oneness of all Creation and love its wisdom.

Yet something within the heart of the cosmos stirs new life within Her—a new promise of a different future, a new unveiling and a new possibility. It can happen, if only they can make a different choice.

Ah! But she is so tired. She turns away from the two beings, from the engineered perfection which has taken them away from their souls.

Suddenly, the hybrid reveals its face to Her, and she can see a glimmer of Herself in the creature's memory. Now she remembers that once she was sitting in a fragrant garden, long before descending into the end of darkness. She remembers Herself as Inanna, Demeter, Mary Magdalene, and Sophia. And as she remembers Her descent and Her cry to the Light, she knows that the path to ascension is still open and that a new dawn is possible.

SELECTED REFERENCES

Allen, J 2023, *Dark Aeon: Transhumanism and the War against Humanity*, Skyhorse Publishing, New York

Bizzi, N 2020, *Egypt and Eleusinian Mysteries*, Aurora Boreale, Copenhagen

Bledsoe, C 2023, *The UFO of God. The Extraordinary True Story of Chris Bledsoe*, David Broadwell,

Braden, G 2025, *Pure Human: The Hidden Truth of our Divinity, Power and Destiny*, Hay House, Carlsbad, California.

Clarke, N 2021, *Baba Yaga. Slavic Earth Goddess*, Moon Books, London

Conner, M 2010, *Voices of Gnosticism*, Bardic Press

Dalleur, P 2021, 'Fatima pictures and testimonials: in depth analysis', *Scientia et Fides*, Pontifical University of the holy Cross, Rome

Davies, SL 1980, *The Revolt of the Widows: The Social World of the Apocryphal Acts of the Apostles*, Feffer & Simon, London

Douka, K, Efstratiou, N, Hald, MM, Henriksen, PS, Karetsou, A 2017, 'Dating Knossos and the arrival of the earliest Neolithic in the southern Aegean', *Antiquity*. 91(356), pp. 304-321. doi:10.15184/aqy.2017.29

Fox, M, Sheldrake, R 1996, *The Physics of Angels: Exploring the Realms Where Science and Science Meet*, Monkfish Book Publishing, New York

Hancock, G 2006, *Supernatural: Meetings with the Ancient Teachers of Mankind*, Arrow Ltd – Mass Market

Hesemann, M 2000, *The Fatima Secret (Whitley Strieber's Hidden Agendas)*, Dell, New York

Hoffman, G-L 2003, *The Secret Dowry of Eve*, Park Street Press, Rochester, US

Hughey, J, Paschou, P, Drineas, P et al 2013, 'A European population in Minoan Bronze Age Crete', *Nature Communications*, 4, 1861, https://doi.org/10.1038/ncomms2871

Kripal, JJ 2017, *Secret Body: Erotic and Esoteric Currents in the History of Religions*, University of Chicago Press

Kujawa, J 2022, *The Other Goddess: Mary Magdalene and the Goddesses of Eros and Secret Knowledge*, Haniel Press, Fort Lauderdale, US

Leloup, J-Y 2002, *The Gospel of Mary Magdalene*, Inner Traditions, Rochester, US

Mack, J 1994, *Abduction: Human Encounters with Aliens*, Scribner's, New York

MacRae, G.W (trans.) n.d., *Thunder, Perfect Mind*, The Gnostic Society Library, http://www.gnosis.org/naghamm/thunder.html

Mead, GRS 2017, translation of *Pistis Sophia*, Mockingbird Press

Pagels, E 1989, *The Gnostic Gospels*, Vintage Books, New York

Palmer, S 2004, *Aliens Adored. Rael's UFO Religion*, Rutgers University Press, New Brunswick, US

Pasulka, DW 2019, *American Cosmic*, Oxford University Press, Oxford

Pasulka, DW 2023, *Encounters: Experiences with Nonhuman Intelligences*, St. Martin's Essentials, London

Rigoglioso, M 2021 *The Mystery Tradition of Immaculate Conception*, Bear & Company, Rochester, US

Seiler, S 2013, "DNA analysis unearths origins of Minoans, the first major European civilization", *UW News*, viewed 24 May 2025 https://www.washington.edu/news/2013/05/14/dna-analysis-unearths-origins-of-minoans-the-first-major-european-civilization/

Sheldrake, R 2012, *The Science Delusion. Freeing the Spirit of Enquiry*, Coronet Books, London

Sitchin, Z 2015, *The Anunnaki Chronicles*, J Sitchin (Ed), Bear & Company, Rochester, US

Strassman, R, Wojtowicz, S, Eduardo Luna, L, Frecska, E 2008, *Inner Paths to Outer Space: Journeys to Alien Worlds through Psychedelics and Other Spiritual Technologies*, Park Street Press, Rochester, US

Urbain, T 2025, "AI is learning to lie, scheme, and threaten its creators," *Tech Xplore*, https://techxplore.com/news/2025-06-ai-scheme-threaten-creators.html

Vallée, J 1993, *Passport to Magonia: On UFOs Folklore and Parallel Worlds*, Contemporary Books, Chicago

Vernon, M 2022, *Spiritual Intelligence in Seven Steps*, Iff Books, UK

Evelyn-White, HG 2011, translation of *Homeric Hymn to Demeter*, Oaklight Publishing

Wolkstein, D, Kramer, SN 1983, translation of *The Descent of Inanna* from *Inanna, Queen of Heaven and Earth: Her Stories and Hymns from Sumer*, Harper & Row, New York

Zelazo, S 2022, *The Way of Inanna: A Heroine's Guide to Living Unapologetically*, Haniel Press, Fort Lauderdale, US

ENDNOTES

1 Duncan, R 18 June 2024, "Angels or aliens? Some researchers say Vatican hold UFO secrets", *United States Conference of Catholic Bishops*, viewed May 2025 https://www.usccb.org/news/2024/angels-or-aliens-some-researchers-say-vatican-archives-hold-ufo-secrets

2 St. Theresa of Avila 2007, Interior Castle, trans. E. Allison Peers, Dover Publications, Garden City, NY

3 Pasulka, DW 2023, *Encounters: Experiences with Nonhuman Intelligences*, St. Martin's Essentials, London

4 Science Council, "Our Definition of Science", viewed 5/24/2025, https://sciencecouncil.org/about-science/our-definition-of-science/

5 Sheldrake, R 2012, *The Science Delusion. Freeing the Spirit of Enquiry*, Coronet Books, London

6 Ellis, C 2023 "Science communicators need to stop telling everybody the Universe is a meaningless void", *Conversation*, viewed September 2024 https://theconversation.com/profiles/chris-ellis-1440038

7 Allen, J 2023 *Dark Aeon: Transhumanism and the War Against Humanity*, War Room Books,

8 Pilat, A 2023 "Meet Agnieszka Pilat: The artist creating portraits for the machines of the future", euronews.culture, viewed 9/22/2024, https://www.euronews.com/culture/2023/06/02/meet-agnieszka-pilat-the-artist-creating-portraits-for-the-machines-of-the-future

9 McArthur, N 2023 "Gods in the machine", *Conversation*, viewed 9/18/2024, https://theconversation.com/profiles/neil-mcarthur-548397

10 McArthur, N 202, "Gods in the machine", *Conversation*, viewed 9/18/2024,

11 Vernon, M 2022 *Spiritual Intelligence in Seven Steps*, Iff Books, UK

12 MacRae, G.W (trans.) n.d., *Thunder, Perfect Mind*, The Gnostic Society Library, viewed 5/22/2025, http://www.gnosis.org/naghamm/thunder.html

13 Pagels, E 1989 *The Gnostic Gospels*, Vintage Books, New York, p.55

14 Seiler, S 2013 'DNA analysis unearths origins of Minoans, the first major European civilization', *UW News*, viewed 24 May 2025 https://www.washington.edu/news/2013/05/14/dna-analysis-unearths-origins-of-minoans-the-first-major-european-civilization/

15 Keller, M.L 2018 "The myriad faces, marvelous powers, and theaology of Greek Goddesses" in Goddesses in (eds) Beavis, M.A and Hwang, H Goddesses in Myth, History and Culture, Mago Books, San Bernardo, CA, p.144,

16 Leloup, J-Y *2002 The Gospel of Mary Magdalene*, Inner Traditions, Rochester, p.37

17 Leloup, J-Y *2002 The Gospel of Mary Magdalene*, Inner Traditions, Rochester, p.35

18 Jung, C.G 1992 *Two Essays on Analytical Psychology*, Second Edition, Collected Works of C.G. Jung, Routledge, London,

19 Mead, G.R.S. 2012 *Pistis Sophia*, Stuart Publishing LLC, US.

ABOUT THE AUTHOR

Dr. Joanna Kujawa is a scholar, spiritual detective, and the author of *Alien Goddess: UFOs, AI, and the Goddesses of Ascension* and *The Other Goddess: Mary Magdalene and the Goddesses of Eros and Secret Knowledge*. She received her BA and MA from the Pontifical Institute for Medieval Studies at the University of Toronto, Canada, and her PhD from Monash University, Melbourne, Australia.

As an active academic for over 20 years, she uses her scholarly training to investigate topics other academics often pass over such as what is the nature of UFO experiences? Is there a connection between AI, UFO, and the esoteric Goddess Traditions of Inanna, the Eleusinian Mysteries, *The Gospel of Mary Magdalene*, and the *Pistis Sophia*?

Her book, *The Other Goddess*, is also available in Mandarin. She is a regular guest on many popular shows and is featured on Season 4 of the acclaimed Magical Egypt series.

https://www.joannakujawa.com/